The Prayer Driven Life

The Prayer Driven Life

ROBERT OH

WIPF & STOCK · Eugene, Oregon

THE PRAYER DRIVEN LIFE

Wipf & Stock
An Imprint of Wipf and Stock Publishers
199 W. 8th Ave., Suite 3
Eugene, OR 97401
www.wipfandstock.com

ISBN 13: 978-1-61097-602-2

Manufactured in the U.S.A.

This book is dedicated to Dr. David Yonggi Cho
A prayer warrior who transformed the world on his knees.

&

Dr. Paul HJ Kim
who introduced me to the world of spiritual giants.

It is Christ who died, and furthermore is also risen,
who is even at the right hand of God,
who also makes intercession for us.

—ROM. 8:34

Contents

Introduction ix

PART I: TO BE LIKE JESUS 1

Day 1: Why pray?

Day 2: What is prayer?

Day 3: Your attitude toward prayer

Day 4: Can a sinner like me pray?

PART II: TO PRAY LIKE JESUS 22

Day 5: Is there order in prayer?

Day 6: Prayer is petition—ASK, Part I

Day 7: Prayer is petition—ASK, Part II

Day 8: Topical prayer

Day 9: The Ripple prayer

Day 10: Prayer is devotion—SEEK

Day 11: Prayer conquers over your flesh & mind

Day 12: Tabernacle prayer, Part I

Day 13: Tabernacle prayer, Part II

Day 14: Tabernacle prayer, Part III

Part III: To Join Jesus in His Prayer 81

Day 15: Prayer is intercession—KNOCK

Day 16: Warfare prayer

Day 17: The Lord's Prayer

Day 18: Fasting prayer

Part IV: Listen and Obey 108

Day 19: God speaks

Day 20: Listen and obey

Day 21: Can you tarry with me an hour?

Appendices 121
Bibliography 127

Introduction

"Far be it from me that I should sin against the Lord
in ceasing to pray for you . . ."

—1 SAM 12:23.

GOD WANTS you to live a supernatural life. One of the main common denominators of great men and women of God is that they were all great prayer warriors. You cannot change the world on your own strength. Unless you humble yourself in prayer, and rely on God's power, you can only do what's humanly possible. At the end of your life you will wonder, "That was it?" Without God, your life will be only earthly, natural and predictable; it won't be supernatural. You reap what you sow. As you begin, I want to invite you to this incredible supernatural life—fashioned by God and through your prayer.

In the early 1990s I was attending a church growth conference hosted by a pastor whose church reached 8,000 at the time. It was considered one of the largest churches in America. For three days he taught us, but there was not one session on prayer or even the mention of prayer. Finally on the last day, at the last session, with only thirty minutes left, I had to raise my hand and ask a question. "Yes, do you have a question?" He acknowledged me. I asked, quite nervously, because there were almost a thousand pastors present, "Sir, you have taught us how to grow a church for the last few days, but you did not mention anything on prayer. Is there room for prayer in your church growth principle?" And what he said in response to my question will forever grieve me. "You can pray all you want, but prayer will not grow a church!" Something died inside of me. I was a young pastor trying to plant a church at that time. I had a vision to plant a healthy, vibrant, praying church that our Lord Jesus himself would be proud of. With great aspiration and excitement I was attending this conference, but I had to walk out of that grandiose building muttering, "But Jesus said that his house is a house of prayer."[1]

Prayer was never meant to be used as a tool to grow a church. It is to be the DNA of a church. When someone says, "My church is not a praying church," what you are really saying is, "My church is not a church yet!" It may be a gathering of Christians, even a large crowd, but don't call it a church. It does not fit Jesus' definition of what a church is.

What Dr. C. Peter Wagner said in my doctorate course is true. "The tragedy of America is that we can grow our churches without God. As a matter of fact, we don't know what to do when God shows up!"[2] Dr. Van Engen of Fuller Theological Seminary argues that in our pursuit of church growth, we have emphasized too much on the "growth" aspect and not enough on "church." It is growing, but is it a church? Not everything that grows is a church.

1. Luke 19:46. Jesus was quoting Isa 56:7, "Even them I will bring to My holy mountain, And make them joyful in My house of prayer. Their burnt offerings and their sacrifices will be accepted on My altar; For My house shall be called a house of prayer for all nations."

2. This was mentioned at Colorado Springs New Life Church. I was taking my Doctor of Ministry course at Fuller Theological Seminary.

In 1996, Dr. Bill Bright challenged many young Christians at a conference to fast and pray 40 days for America. He said that unless America repents, fasts, and prays, God will have to apologize to Sodom and Gomorrah. I took this godly man's challenge seriously. I fasted 40 days and prayed for America in 1998, 1999, and, as I write this book, am finishing my third fast of 40 days.

A church that does not pray is not a church yet. A nation that does not seek God in prayer is not a Christian nation. A prayer-less believer is powerless! A prayer-less nation is powerless as well! That is, each is powerless against the enemy's attack.

This book is written for my churches in Southern California, that they would hold a 21 day Daniel fast and pray for America from September 11 to October 1. The 9/11 tragedy taught us one thing. It wasn't America's high tech defense system that protected us from the enemy's attack all these years. It was God's sovereign hand covering us. Dr. Bill Bright's challenge was prophetic. We've all experienced a little sampling of what Sodom and Gomorrah went through. If America is growing prayer-less churches, we will become a nation full of churches and yet still not a Christian nation. God's hand of protection will lift, not by his choice, but by our rejection of his presence and sin of prayerlessness.[3]

My discouragement turned into joy when I met Dr. David Yonggi Cho of the Yoido Full Gospel Church of Korea for the first time that year. Dr. Paul HJ Kim, my spiritual mentor since 1979, whom I love and respect, became the executive director of Church Growth International

3. 1 Sam 12:23.

(CGI), and through his relationship with Dr. Cho, I had the privilege of spending some private time with him in the Los Angeles area.

I had a burning question for him. I was barely introduced when I asked him a question point blank, "Dr. Cho, what is your secret of church growth?" He graciously smiled and lifted up three fingers. Counting one finger down at a time he said, "First, Prayer. Second, Prayer. And, third, Prayer. That's it!" I was comforted by the fact that Dr. Cho's church was slightly bigger than the other speaker's church—at that time around 750,000—the world's largest church!

Dr. Cho writes this prayer principle in his book entitled *Born to be Blessed*.

> Whenever I go to other nations and teach Church Growth Seminars, the pastors' prime concern is, "What is the major secret of your church growth?" My reply is always the same, "It is prayer." There is no secret for church growth other than prayer. When Christians pray, the work of the Holy Spirit is manifested. The forces of the devil are demolished and circumstances are changed."[4]

That's it! This is the DNA of church in action. The forces of the devil are being demolished, and genuine transformation takes place when the Holy Spirit is at work. That's the church Jesus is talking about. If someone you know is demonized and full of sin, to which church would you take him? A prayer-less church or a praying church? The real issue with the church growth movement in America is not about the growth aspect, but it is really about the essence of a church.

4. Cho, *Born to be Blessed*, 141.

As we were finishing our shopping, in an elevator, Dr. Cho leaned over to me and said, "Pastor Oh, let me share with you a very important fact. The most difficult number to break in church growth is 200,000!" Hmm . . . thank you, Dr. Cho, when I have that problem, I will call you up, sir.

I walked out, I mean I danced my way out, of that elevator. With his encouraging words, I was able to plant five churches within the next 15 years. A few campus churches, at UCLA[5] and USC, one church in a suburb, one in downtown Los Angeles, and one in a government housing project for urban youths. You ask, "So, are they growing?" Yes, they are growing. Some are big and some small numerically. But most importantly, they are all prayer driven churches.[6] I don't think I will ever call Dr. Cho seeking counsel on how to break 200,000, but what he taught me that day, I will treasure forever. The core of the church growth principle is this: praying churches grow! The praying church, regardless of its size of membership, is a gigantic church in God's kingdom.

GETTING THE MOST FROM THIS BOOK

This book, *The Prayer Driven Life*, is designed to take you through a 21 day journey on prayer. While I fasted 40 days this time, I read through 30 books that Dr. Cho wrote on prayer and systematically arranged them with my own teaching, insights and testimonies. The main teaching and outline is from Dr. Cho's books.

5. This church has now joined another denomination.

6. Oikos Declaration: "We are Prayer Driven, Word Based, Spirit Led, Mission Focused disciples influencing our world in Jesus name!" This says it all about who we are.

I wrote this book with you in mind. I have been fasting and praying for you that as you read this book you will be set free from prayerlessness and become a powerful prayer warrior. The Christian life without authentic and life changing prayer is neither authentic nor life changing!

If you are a prayer warrior already, this book will enable you to systematically teach and disciple those you want to train. Learn the principles, use them, and discipline yourself in them and your Christian life will become supernatural. I am so excited for you. Shall we begin this journey together? Let's go.

WHY TWENTY-ONE DAYS OF PRAYER?

The next twenty-one days will absolutely transform your life.

At my church over the years, we have been doing many Daniel Fasts for twenty-one days and saw great results—both corporately as a church and personally as individuals. I learned from a psychologist that the average duration needed for a habit to form is around twenty-one days, especially for a good habit. So, we want to form a good habit of prayer and give it a long enough time for it to become a normal, daily part of us.

Also, many years ago, when I had a major issue I was grappling with God about, I went into an extended fast. The special thing about this fast was that I told God unless he released me from the burden I had, I wouldn't stop fasting. Well, you guessed it. I really, really prayed hard. The realistic goal of being released from fasting was crucial. One day, three days, seven days, and ten days went by, but there was no release from the Lord. I prayed, "God, how many more days?" Twelve, fifteen, seventeen, and twenty days went by but still no sign. I became quite desperate. I stopped praying a civilized and nice Christian-sounding prayer but started crying out to God! "Lord, release me from this burden or else I will die!" Finally, the release came on the morning of the twenty-second day. An incredible peace came into my heart, and I knew God answered my prayer. I had fasted exactly twenty-one days. Then at a later time, I discovered the story of Daniel and how he was released after twenty-one days of praying.

Daniel experienced a breakthrough after praying for twenty-one days. The Prince of Persia was the spiritual force that guided the advancement of the world government. Gabriel had been sent by God, but the Satanic princes, or fallen angels, made war against Gabriel—Satan not wanting Daniel's prayer to be answered. Michael, the Archangel, was called in to assist Gabriel in the battle.

In this story, the angel of the Lord said to Daniel, "Do not fear, Daniel, for from the first day that you set your heart to understand, and to humble yourself before your God, your words were heard; and I have come because of your words. But the prince of the kingdom of Persia withstood me twenty-one days; and behold, Michael, one of the chief princes, came to help me, for I had been left alone there with the kings of Persia."[7]

The prophet Daniel had fasted and prayed for twenty-one days. The length of time necessary for God's spiritual forces to overcome the work of the enemy for Daniel was twenty-one days.[8]

---

7. Dan 10:12–13.
8. Keil-Delitzsch, *Commentary on the Old Testament*, 416–17.

Of course, our mighty God can do it in one second if he desires, but it seems that out of those twenty-one days of waiting on the Lord, God worked on Daniel as much as he was solving Daniel's problem.

BREAKTHROUGH

In the next twenty-one days you will be challenged to have a major breakthrough in your prayer life. You will learn many different patterns of prayer, and each day you will be given an opportunity to practice prayer.

Spend as much time reflecting on what you've learned and practice different kinds of prayer each day. Do not read more than one day at a time. The point of this book is not to read it through but to master the prayer that you are learning each day.

Go ahead and have fun praying and interacting with other people by sharing what you learn. Praying is the most exciting spiritual discipline because it will yield the highest dividend in your life on earth and hereafter. Remember, prayer is what church is about at its core level.

Media Fast. While you are on this journey, I recommend that you go through a media Fast. This means no television, no videos, no DVDs, no movies, etc. Keep your mind focused on God, and spend those redeemed times on prayer.

Daniel Fast. If you want to really experience the cleansing of body and mind, try the Daniel Fast.[9] This means no meat in your diet, but you can have as many vegetables and fruits as you want. Some add fish, and that's fine. Doing this for twenty-one days will cleanse your digestive system and give you more energy and much more focus on prayer.

9. Dan 1:8.

Juice or Water Fast. Are you really serious about experiencing God for the next twenty-one days? Try either a juice or water fast.

FOUR FEATURES TO HELP YOU

At the end of each day's reading, you will find these features to help you.

- An insight to meditate on. True learning takes place by repetition. Repeat the nuggets of truth from each day through out the day. Out of that continuous reflection, the insights will become yours to keep. "The meditation of my heart shall give understanding."[10]

- God's word to heartify. Do not just memorize God's word. Once memorized, put it in your heart—that's what "heartifying" the word is. In French, the word "heart" is the organ that thinks. The psalmist was right when he said, "Your word I have hidden in my heart, that I might not sin against Thee."[11]

- A question to ask. You must act on what you learn. The questions at the end of each day will help you to clarify and apply the truth to your life. "He is not a forgetful hearer but a doer of the word, this one will be blessed in what he does."[12]

- Let Us Pray! These coaching suggestions will help you to pray more effectively. You will be able to pray what you just learned right away. Have fun praying!

10. Ps 49:3b.
11. Ps 119:11.
12. Jas 1:25b.

My Covenant

With the help of the Holy Spirit, I commit the next twenty-one days of my life to prayer to become like Jesus Christ.

_____

Your Name

_____

Partner's Name

_____

Signature

"Two are better than one,
because they have a good reward for their labor.
For if they fall, one will lift up his companion.
But woe to him who is alone when he falls,
for he has no one to help him up."

—ECCL 4:9, 10 (NKJV)

Part I: To Be Like Jesus

DAY 1: WHY PRAY?

"Pray without ceasing.

—1 Thess 5:17

"Prayer does not change God, but it changes us."

—Soren Kierkegaard

You want to be like Jesus.

Why pray? First of all, because you want to be like Jesus. Jesus was a man of prayer before anything else. Every response he made to the people around him was solely at the direction he received from the Father in prayer! Jesus said, "Most assuredly, I say to you, the Son can do nothing of himself, but what he sees the Father do; for whatever he does, the Son also does in like manner."[1]

The victory Jesus Christ won at the cross was first won in the place of fervent prayer in Gethsemane.[2] Therefore, as Dr. Cho puts it, "For Christians, the first priority is prayer; the second priority is prayer; and the third is prayer, too.[3]

1. John 5:19.
2. Chavda, *The Hidden Power of Prayer and Fasting*, 139.
3. Cho, *How to Pray*, 103.

John Maxwell said, "The 'detonator' that churches lack today is prayer. It has the power to ignite the dynamite of the Gospel and powerfully shake the world." You should replace the word 'churches' to 'Christians' and read it once more. Wow! It is a sobering fact. Remember, bombs without detonators are nothing more than dead weights.

Why pray? Secondly, because you need to have intimate fellowship with the Holy Spirit. The Holy Spirit can bless you when you read the Scriptures. The Holy Spirit can direct you as you witness for Christ. The Holy Spirit can anoint you as you share the love of God to others. But if you want to have intimate communion with the Holy Spirit you need to pray.[4] It stems from a simple principle—you cannot have intimacy without communication. Connection is made through communication. Prayer is communication with God through the Holy Spirit.

Therefore, the success of your Christian life largely depends on your relationship with the Holy Spirit. He is the Comforter our Lord Jesus promised as he ascended to heaven. Until Jesus comes back in his glory, the Holy Spirit is the God-head whom you have access to in order to communicate with God.[5]

Your prayer life begins with recognizing that the Holy Spirit is a person who is seeking an intimate relationship with you. Your Christian life is a life managed and led by the Holy Spirit. Without the Holy Spirit, you cannot receive

4. Cho, *Prayer: Key to Revival*, 44.

5. John 14:25–26: "These things I have spoken to you while being present with you. But the Helper, the Holy Spirit, whom the Father will send in my name, he will teach you all things, and bring to your remembrance all things that I said to you."

Jesus Christ as your Savior, nor can you offer true prayer, genuine praise or inspired worship to God.

Who is the Holy Spirit? AW Tozer said, "Spell this out in capital letters: THE HOLY SPIRIT IS A PERSON. He is not enthusiasm. He is not courage. He is not energy. He is not the personification of all good qualities, like Jack Frost is the personification of cold weather. Actually, the Holy Spirit is not the personification of anything. He has individuality. He is one being and not another. He has will and intelligence. He has hearing. He has knowledge and sympathy and ability to love and see and think. He can hear, speak, desire, grieve and rejoice. He is a Person."

The Holy Spirit is the Spirit of God.

The Spirit who has knowledge.

The Spirit who has emotions.

The Sprit who has a will.

The Spirit who desires communication.

After such recognition, you must seek daily fellowship with him. Why don't you pray this *Prayer of Invitation* now?[6]

> O living God, we acknowledge, welcome, accept and trust the Holy Spirit who does great work as he abides in us. Fill us with the Holy Spirit this very moment, and help us so that our lives can glorify your name. Help us to live in continued fellowship with the Holy Spirit so that we may live victoriously from now until the day we enter heaven. In Jesus name I pray, Amen.

6. Cho, *The Nature of God: Who is God . . . Really?*, 150.

For relationship sake. You can object and ask, "Isn't God omnipotent to do things for me before I ask?" Yes, but at the core of it, your prayer is not about getting things from him, but getting close to him. Also, the Word of God tells us to pray without ceasing [7] and seek his counsel daily. This is because you cannot keep a healthy relationship without continuous and open communication. In the same way, you cannot keep a good relationship with God without talking to him daily.

What is the proper motive for prayer? It is to communicate with God and express our love to him. You direct your prayers to God because your first motive is to have a relationship with him, not to get things from him.

For winning sake. Simply put, "You cannot win without praying!" The spiritual war rages on daily whether we want it or not. It is like saying, "You cannot win a battle if you don't fight!" "You cannot win a swim competition without jumping into the water!" "You cannot win a surfing competition upon the mountain!" "You cannot win the Tour de France in Hawaii!" Should I go on? The point is that you need to do and be where it counts.

The apostle Paul said to the church in Ephesus, "Finally, my brethren, be strong in the Lord and in the power of his might. Put on the whole armor of God, that you may be able to stand against the wiles of the devil . . . praying always with all prayer and supplication in the Spirit, being watchful to this end with all perseverance and supplication for all the saints." [8]

7. 1 Thess 5:17.
8. Eph 6:10–11, 18.

The world is ruled by the enemy, and the Word of God says that he seeks to devour us like a roaring lion.[9] Then, how can we walk out to such a hostile environment without getting ready for it? Martin Luther, the reformer, once said that he prayed one hour a day to go through the day and three hours a day to be victorious over the devil. Conditioning ourselves to pray daily is crucial, like an athlete who is in constant training. The Bible tells us to "exercise yourself toward godliness." [10]

All the great world class achievers did not accomplish them casually or accidentally. Without discipline, you cannot really be good at anything. Ask Tiger Woods if he accidentally became a good golfer, and he would shake his head in disbelief. He won't even answer you. You see, it is the same with prayer. You cannot casually become a prayer warrior—you have to give yourself to prayer and discipline yourself to pray. That's what our Lord Jesus did. And I want to become like Jesus. What about you?

Day 1: To Be Like Jesus

An insight to meditate on: I want to be like Jesus by praying.
God's word to heartify: "Pray without ceasing." 1 Th. 5:17

A question to ask: How can I plan my daily schedule to give more time for prayer?

Let us pray: Spend some time in prayer inviting the Holy Spirit into your life. Recognize him and honor him in your prayer. Talk to him as you would with your loved ones. Remember the Holy Spirit is a person.

9. 1 Pet 5:8.
10. 1 Tim 4:7.

DAY 2: WHAT IS PRAYER?

"Praying always with all prayer and supplication in the Spirit, being watchful to this end with all perseverance and supplication for all the saints."

—EPH. 6:18

"To pray is to change. Prayer is the central avenue God uses to transform us. If we are unwilling to change, we will abandon prayer as a noticeable characteristic of our lives."

—RICHARD FOSTER

Prayer gives life to your spiritual body.

Prayer is your spiritual breath. Just as the Bible is nutrition for your spirit, prayer is the breathing of your spirit. You can go a few days without food, but try five minutes without breathing. Spiritually, your prayer is that much more important. Spiritual death takes place either by not eating or not breathing. Many well-meaning Christians today die gasping for air yet their spiritual stomach is full. Of course, you should not lack either—it's a both/and issue, not an either/or. As a Christian, you need both the Word of God and prayer.

Prayer gives life. The Bible tells us to pray without ceasing. Jesus prayed so regularly and after prayer was so full of life that his disciples wanted to pray just like him. As Jesus was praying in a certain place, one of his disciples came and made a request of him. "Lord, teach us to pray."[11] It's not that he did not know how to pray. As a Jew he knew how to

11. Luke 11:1.

pray. But he wanted to pray like Jesus. What he was saying was, "Lord, how do you pray like that? It is so different than our religious leaders' ritualistic prayers. I am not used to your kind of prayer, Lord. Teach me to pray just like you!" That's what he meant because he noticed something different about Jesus' prayer.

Jesus' prayer gives life—to himself and to those around him. Prayer is our spiritual breath. Let's start breathing! Give life to your spiritual body!

Prayer is having a conversation with God. The Bible says that Jesus went out to the mountain to pray and continued all night in prayer.[12] Jesus was having conversation with God. He knew to whom he was praying. He did not turn prayer into a religious duty but a relational reality. Jesus was really, really, really talking to God. I mean—really. I will say it again. Jesus was *really* talking to God!

Jesus warns his disciples not to make prayer a religious activity.

> And when you pray, you shall not be like the hypocrites. For they love to pray standing in the synagogues and on the corners of the streets, that they may be seen by men. Assuredly, I say to you, they have their reward. But you, when you pray, go into your room, and when you have shut your door, pray to your Father who is in the secret place; and your Father who sees in secret will reward you openly. And when you pray, do not use vain repetitions as the heathen do. For they think that they will be heard for their many words.[13]

12. Luke 6:12.
13. Matt. 6:5–7.

Don't use religious jargon when you pray. Prayer is speaking to God using our own words and thoughts. It's as natural as talking to your loved ones over a nice cup of tea. Have a nice time with God when you pray. Take a prayer walk with God. Talk to him and have awesome fellowship with him. The Holy Spirit desires that intimate fellowship with you. Make him happy. Go ahead, talk to him, pour out your heart to him, confess your love to him, and watch him smile over you.

Prayer is worship. Prayer is an act of worship to a living God. The moment you turn prayer into a ritual, you turn God into an idol. You see, an idol is an object, and you do not have a relationship with an object. God is not an object. He is alive, and he wants to have a real relationship with you. So, when you pray, talk to him and do not turn that precious time into a ritual.

Prayer is your spiritual muscle. Prayer is a powerful weapon against the advances of Satan. The Bible says that the prayer of faith will "save the sick, and the Lord will raise him up. Pray for one another, that you may be healed."[14] What Satan is doing to destroy can be defended and fought back in prayer.

Do you remember Samson? Satan had him good and tied him to two posts of the temple of God's enemies. He made his final prayer, "O Lord God, remember me, I pray! Strengthen me, I pray, just this once, O God, that I may with one blow take vengeance on the Philistines for my two eyes![15] This Scripture makes it clear that Samson did not rely on his own muscle strength. He was praying to God

14. James 5:15–16.
15. Judg. 16:28.

to activate his spiritual muscle. When you pray, you put on God's muscle and accomplish supernatural work. The Christian life is a supernatural life. Start pumping that spiritual muscle!

I sometimes do push ups while I am praying aloud just to remind myself that as I pray I am building up my spiritual muscle. Try it—it's a healthy way to pray! By learning to do prayer jogging, I finished two marathons this year—a half marathon and a full marathon. That's 26.2 miles of praying! Hallelujah! I tell my friends that my spiritual body looks like our governor Arnold! Imagine that! What does your spiritual body look like?

Battles continue. You must keep awake and pray for victory for yourselves and for your fellow Christians. The Bible says that the enemy wants to overpower you. In the natural realm, he is stronger than you. That's why you need to put on the prayer muscle which is supernatural. "Be sober, be vigilant; because your adversary the devil walks about like a roaring lion, seeking whom he may devour."[16]

Rely on the Holy Spirit. If you feel spiritually weak, then you must rely on the Holy Spirit as you pray. "Likewise the Holy Spirit also helps in our weaknesses. For we do not know what we should pray for as we ought, but the Spirit himself makes intercession for us with groanings which cannot be uttered." [17]

Prayer is the key. Prayer is the key to all your problems. No matter what your problems may be, you must take them to God in prayer to find solutions. God has solutions to all of your problems. So, be anxious for nothing, but in

16. 1 Pet. 5:8.
17. Rom. 8:26.

everything by prayer and supplication, with thanksgiving, let your requests be made known to God. [18] Amen?

God promises to answer all of your sincere prayers. "Ask, and it will be given to you; seek, and you will find; knock, and it will be opened to you. For everyone who asks receives, and he who seeks finds, and to him who knocks it will be opened."[19]

Can you imagine taking a test with an answer sheet in front of you? That's what praying provides when you face problems. Pray deeply and you will know the answer to your problems. So, going through the test is easy and anxiety free. Praise the Lord.

Day 2: To Be Like Jesus

An insight to meditate on: Prayer gives life to your spiritual body!

God's word to heartify: "Be anxious for nothing, but in everything by prayer and supplication, with thanksgiving, let your requests be made known to God" Phil. 4:6

A question to ask: Are you as desperate about prayer as someone under water gasping for air? In both cases, the end result is same—physical death or spiritual death. Think deeply about it today and take a long breath.

Let us pray: Let's pray desperately like a man under water. Then take a prayer walk with God and talk to him. Share your heart out! He is listening—and he is smiling!

18. Phil 4:6.
19. Matt 7:7, 8.

DAY 3: YOUR ATTITUDE TOWARD PRAYER

*"But seek first the kingdom of God and his righteousness, and
all these things shall be added to you."*

—MATT 6:33

*"I have been driven many times to my knees by the overwhelm-
ing conviction that I had nowhere else to go. My own wisdom
and that of those about me seemed insufficient for the day."*

—ABRAHAM LINCOLN

Don't just pray. Saturate your life in prayer!

Saturate your life in prayer![20] What a concept! I personally witnessed this concept in action while at Guatemala. I
was accompanying Dr. Cho on his crusade. There was an
exciting reception with both the present and the former
Presidents of Guatemala attending the service. They honored him with a gift and special music which lasted for more
than an hour. I was very happy for him, but I noticed that he
was not very pleased about all that was taking place.

At the end of the first night Dr. Cho called the organizer
and graciously said, "Brother, I am not here to be honored
by the people, but to preach the Gospel to them. Please let
me have a private room to pray before the service tomorrow.
Today I prayed for many hours to bring the Word of God,
but while you were celebrating, all that spiritual energy was
consumed within me." Wow, talk about being focused on
the task God has given him. Dr. Cho was right, he wasn't

20. Schuller and Cho, *Expand Your Horizon: How to Make Your Faith Work!*, 45.

there to be honored by the Presidents, although that was very nice, but to serve the King of kings on a much greater mission—to preach the Gospel.

The next day, Dr. Cho was in waiting room while the others were worshipping. He has been preaching for forty-five years. He built the world's largest church. And yet, he prayed, "Oh Holy Spirit please use me tonight. Without you, there is nothing I can do. There is nothing I have that I can give to these precious people. Holy Spirit I welcome you and depend on you." He was like a little child desperately seeking daddy's strong arm to come around him and lift him up. I saw a childlike purity in his prayer.

Dr. Cho was totally saturated in prayer. That night in Guatemala, God moved powerfully and touched many lives—especially mine. I walked away from that meeting with a lesson on prayer I will not forget: don't just pray, but saturate your whole being in prayer. That's how Jesus prayed at Gethsemane—his sweat became blood![21]

Pray God's will. You must pray fervently in faith according to God's will. John writes, "Now this is the confidence that we have in him, that if we ask anything according to his will, he hears us." [22] Turn God's will for you into a prayer. But you must pray in faith if you want God to answer you. The apostle James writes, "Let him ask in faith, with no doubting, for he who doubts is like a wave of the sea driven and tossed by the wind. For let not that man suppose that he will receive anything from the Lord; he is a double-minded man, unstable in all his ways."[23]

---

21. Luke 22:44.
22. 1 John 5:14.
23. Jas 1:6–8.

Did you know that it is God's will for you to prosper?[24] God loves you and he wants you to prosper. So, when you are praying for prosperity, don't feel like you are being selfish. Pray for what God wants in your life with faith—that's what praying God's will is. Now, having said that, let me ask you another question. Can you selfishly ask God to prosper you? Absolutely! I think more people pray for prosperity selfishly than not. That prayer, however, God will not answer, because it is out of the flesh and not from faith. Greed stands between you and the true prosperity God wants you to have.

You must learn to pray sincerely without greed. "You lust and do not have. You murder and covet and cannot obtain. You ask and do not receive, because you ask amiss, that you may spend it on your pleasures."[25]

Let me expound on this point a little further with another example. Does God want you to have a fantastic marriage? Yes, it is God's will for you to have a great marriage. You can ask God for a great marriage according to his will in faith, and he will answer you. Just like that. It's that easy! However, as you are praying, contrary to your words, if your desire for a good marriage is all about your selfish, carnal pleasure, out of competitiveness to the couple next door, and for your own comfort and peace—never mind about your spouse—then he will not answer you. As a matter of fact, God will send you and your marriage through a few boot camp experiences to correct your heart and your perspective on your marriage and your spouse.

24. Deut 29:9.
25. Jas 4:2–3.

Pray in Jesus' name. You must pray to the Father in the name of Jesus Christ. Jesus said, "I say to you, whatever you ask the Father in my name he will give you."[26] Do you pray in Jesus' name? You should! That's what Jesus taught us to do. Over the last two thousand years, strange traditions of praying have evolved. Some pray in the names of saints. Some end their prayer by saying, "By the power of the cross." Some even carry a little statue of their favorite saints for prayer! That's not a biblical way of praying to God.

One high school student, who just became a born-again Christian, at a Christian banquet organized by the school led a prayer for the meal. When he was done, since he did not know how to end it, he said, "And Lord that's it!" Then he looked at the wide-eyed guests and said, "Now, let's eat!" It was cute because it was out of ignorance. But doing something contrary to what Jesus has taught us is not cute.

So, when you pray—pray in Jesus' name!

Forgiveness. You must forgive others before you pray to God who already forgave you. "And whenever you stand praying, if you have anything against anyone, forgive him, that your Father in heaven may also forgive you your trespasses." [27]

Praying without forgiving is like trying to write out a check from an account that has no funds in it. It's like charging a credit card that has already reached its limit. You do not have the resource to draw from. Your forgiveness fills up your treasure box in heaven and increases your spending limit on earth.

26. John 16:23b.
27. Mark 11:25.

Seek God's kingdom. You must seek God's kingdom when you pray. Jesus said, "Seek first the kingdom of God and his righteousness, and all these things shall be added to you."[28] Things being added to you is automatic when you are focused on seeking God's kingdom. Which is better? Asking Bill Gates for a new computer or seeking to become the CEO of Microsoft? When you become the CEO, a limitless number of computers is yours. Seek the giver not the gifts.

Testimony. I was twenty-two years old when I married, and we needed a new car. Of course as a young couple, we wanted to have a nice sporty sedan. But the church we were attending needed a mini-van to pick up a bunch of kids for Sunday School every week. So, one day I took my wife's old white Mustang and traded it in for a new Astro mini-van, without asking her permission. I took the "two shall become one" too literally. Yes, I still hear from her about it twenty-one years later. Every time a white Mustang passes us on the freeway, I feel a very distinctive stare from my right side and sometimes my kids will say, "Dad, how could you?"

Back then, it wasn't fashionable for a twenty-two-year old man to drive a mini-van. I don't think it is fashionable now either. Anyways, since we did not have much money, what we bought was a stripped down version. My company bought it and converted it into a working van. That meant no automatic windows, no air-conditioning, no carpet, no nothing. It was basically a large tin can sitting on a six-cylinder engine. But I was happy because I was able to give a ride to a bunch of cute children each week. We utilized that van well for his kingdom.

28. Matt 6:33.

Ten years later when it became a classic—it was the first-year model of the Astro van—the Lord spoke to me one day when I was praying. By this time I had become a pastor of a new church plant and was going through some financial difficulties. The Holy Spirit said to me, "I am giving you a new car; give your old van to a needy pastor." Just like that, a new car was released to me. Praise God!

A few weeks later, I handed over my van key to a pastor from a Navajo reservation who desperately needed a car for his family, and I received a new key for my brand new van from a businessman who did not even attend our church. He was one of the church founding member's boss. No one asked him for it, but God gave him a desire to bless his worker's pastor with a new car. You see, God can do whatever he wants because he is God.

Yes, I bought a brand new Astro mini-van. But this time, because the big boss paid for it, I bought a luxury version with air-conditioning, automatic windows, and carpet! Hallelujah!

Seek God's kingdom first—good things are coming to you!

Day 3: To Be Like Jesus

An insight to meditate on: Saturate yourself in prayer!

God's word to heartify: "Seek first the kingdom of God and his righteousness, and all these things shall be added to you." Matt 6:33

A question to ask: What must I do to saturate my life with prayer? Am I seeking God's kingdom or am I building my own? Whom have I not forgiven yet? What keeps me from having fervent prayers?

Let us pray: Intensity and fervency are crucial in prayer—especially when you are desiring a breakthrough in certain aspects of your life. Shout to the Lord and the Jericho of your life will fall. "The people shouted with a great shout, that the wall fell down flat. Then the people went up into the city, every man straight before him, and they took the city."[29]

DAY 4: CAN A SINNER LIKE ME PRAY?

"There is therefore now no condemnation to those who are in Christ Jesus . . ."

—ROM 8:1A

"The power of prayer is not in the one praying but in the One who hears our prayers."

—MAX LUCADO

Everyone is invited to pray.

Can a sinner like me pray? Yes, in fact the very first prayer for all sinners is to accept Jesus Christ as your Lord and Savior. Then, you will pray an unlimited number of prayers afterwards. Christians are saved but still sinners. You will sin until you die. You are saved but you sin. That makes you a saved sinner. Therefore, a saved sinner must pray!

29. Josh 6:20b.

Many born-again Christians suffer from guilt and shame of sins committed both in the present and in the past. Knowing this, our enemy, the devil, condemns and accuses us so that we won't approach God and try be closer to him. The Bible tells us plainly that, "There is none righteous, no, not one. For all have sinned and fall short of the glory of God."[30] You see, sin is a condition before it is an action. You are a sinner even before you commit certain acts of sin. No one is righteous before our God. God does not love us because we are righteous and sinless. He offers us salvation from that guilt and shame. God offered his Son to die on the cross on our behalf. God's grace and his salvation are available to all of us who are willing to accept these gifts.

Many years ago in America, President Andrew Jackson pardoned Mr. George Wilson from capital punishment for shooting and killing a mail thief. However, Mr. Wilson refused to be pardoned. The Supreme Court ruled that although a pardon was given, because it was refused, the letter of pardon did not have power over that individual's right. Mr. Wilson was executed. In the same way, Jesus forgave all of our sins and yet some people live as the accused waiting to be executed.

The Word of God says clearly that we are pardoned, and therefore we are not under judgment and punishment. "If we confess our sins, he is faithful and just to forgive us our sins and to cleanse us from all unrighteousness."[31]

A sin is a sin, small or great. To God a sin is a sin—period. And when you sin, you are a sinner. Jesus forgave

30. Rom 3:10, 23.
31. 1 John 1:9.

a woman caught in an adulterous act,[32] and people at that time wanted to stone her according to the law. Jesus turned to them and said, "Whoever is without sin throw the first stone!" Who can throw that stone? There was none who was sinless.

Jesus also forgave a criminal who was being crucified next to him.[33] Although the law rightly punished him for his sin, our Lord forgave the sinner. The Bible describes how sin can manifest in our lives: "Now the works of the flesh are evident, which are: adultery, fornication, uncleanness, lewdness, idolatry, sorcery, hatred, contentions, jealousies, outbursts of wrath, selfish ambitions, dissensions, heresies, envy, murders, drunkenness, revelries, and the like; of which I tell you beforehand, just as I also told you in time past, that those who practice such things will not inherit the kingdom of God."[34]

Sure, I did not commit adultery or murder anyone, but I was jealous over my friend's iPod which had a greater memory than mine. According to the word, because I committed a sin of jealousy I cannot inherit the kingdom of God. How can anyone be saved then? That is the point, isn't it? You can never inherit the kingdom of God on your own. You need Jesus as your Lord and Savior, and with him next to you, you can walk right through those pearly gates in heaven. Hallelujah!

We must approach God with confidence knowing that he does not accuse us as a sinner because of what Jesus did on the cross for us. "There is therefore now no condemna-

32. John 8:3–11.
33. Luke 23:33–43.
34. Gal 5:19–21.

tion to those who are in Christ Jesus, who do not walk according to the flesh, but according to the Spirit. For the law of the Spirit of life in Christ Jesus has made me free from the law of sin and death.' [35]

If you have never accepted Christ as Lord and Savior, then why don't you pray this prayer now.

Sinner's Prayer [36]

Oh beloved Christ, I am a sinner.
I do not know where I came from or why I live.
I do not know where I am headed.
But I have been called by you and I want to accept
Your invitation of salvation in faith.
Cleanse me with the blood of the cross. You have died for me.
You have been resurrected for me. I accept you as my Lord and Savior.
Guide me until the day of my last breath.
Thank you for saving me, Jesus.
Holy Spirit come and help me to live as a new person all the days of my life.
I pray all this in the name of Jesus Christ.
Amen.

If you prayed this prayer for the first time in your life, welcome to the Oikos of God. 'Oikos' means 'family' in Greek.

---

35. Rom 8:1, 2.

36. Cho, *A Bible Study for New Christians*, 1997, inside cover. *Adopted with my own words.

Day 4: To Be Like Jesus

An insight to meditate on: You are a child of God; approach the throne of God confidently in prayer.

God's word to heartify: "There is therefore now no condemnation to those who are in Christ Jesus . . ." Rom 8:1

A question to ask: Don't let the enemy condemn you. It was never your own righteousness from the beginning. Admit that you are still a sinner. Then, how can you protect your heart from the enemy's accusation? Write out a list of all the things that the enemy has been accusing you of and burn it as you pray for freedom from bondage.

Let us pray: Let's pray to God as our Father. You are now a member of God's family. Pray with confidence that God will hear your prayer, as a good father to his children. If you have accepted Christ today, make a prayer of dedication to the Christian life.

Part II: To Pray Like Jesus

DAY 5: IS THERE ORDER IN PRAYER?

"Ask . . . Seek . . . Knock . . ."

—Matt 7:7

"Asking God to give us our daily bread should not encourage us to stand around waiting for it to fall from heaven."

—John Wesley

OUR GOD is the God of order: cosmos not chaos!
The world was chaotic in the beginning. Then God showed up, speaking order into it—turning chaos into cosmos—an orderly universe. He put the sun, the moon, and the stars in their place. He placed the water and put fish in it. He placed the sky and put birds in it. He placed the earth and put vegetation and animals in it. God loves the cosmos and dislikes chaos.

So you ask, "Is there order in prayer?" Of course, the answer is *yes*. There is order in everything, including the way we communicate. You wouldn't want anybody to come up to you and start asking for things as soon as he or she starts talking, would you? That's exactly how God feels when his children come to him and start reading down their shopping list.

Let's put some order in our prayer. Let's experience cosmos prayer!

First, when you pray, start with praise and worship. The Bible says that God considered King David as a man after his own heart.[1] Why? Read some of the Psalms he wrote. King David learned to worship God and praised him in the midst of difficulties and trials. Even when his own son was chasing him to kill him, he made that whole episode into a prayer and turned it into a song of praise: "Lord, how they have increased who trouble me! Many are they who rise up against me. Many are they who say of me, 'There is no help for him in God.' But you, O Lord, are a shield for me, my glory and the One who lifts up my head."[2] Wow, he really understood the order of prayer.

So let's start your prayer like this: "Dear God, I thank you for your grace and praise you for your goodness, especially in loving me enough to save me through the blood of Jesus Christ. I thank you for the work of the Holy Spirit in my life."

It's like raising children. If one child always has a thankful heart and the other an ungrateful heart—although they are both loved equally—the one with the right attitude will be blessed more by his or her parents.

Second, you confess your sins before God. We have to recognize the fact that we are sinners before the Lord. The prophet Isaiah recognized that he was a sinner as he stood before the presence of God's glory. "Woe is me, for I am undone! Because I am a man of unclean lips, and I dwell in the midst of a people of unclean lips; for my eyes have seen the King, the Lord of hosts."[3] You should have the same kind

---

1. Acts 13:22.
2. Ps 3:1–3.
3. Isa 6:5.

of attitude in approaching the throne of God by confessing your sins before God.

Third, you ask. "Ask, and it will be given to you."[4] Jesus asked Bartimaeus the blind, "What do you want me to do for you?"[5] Why wouldn't Jesus know that this blind man stumbling on his way to see Jesus would want to receive sight more than anything else? Of course, this blind man wants sight! But Jesus wants to hear from him what his request is. In the same way our Lord wants you to verbalize your prayer requests to him.

Fourth, you thank God for the answer he is going to give. "Be anxious for nothing, but in everything by prayer and supplication, with thanksgiving, let your requests be made known to God; and the peace of God, which surpasses all understanding, will guard your hearts and minds through Christ Jesus."[6] Pray until all the anxiety regarding those prayer requests disappear. And when you enter into that place of peace, you must learn to thank God for answered prayer. Let me tell you a little secret: "Thank God in advance!"

When God overthrew the Egyptian army, Miriam the prophetess, sister of Aaron, took the timbrel in her hand, and all the women went out after her with dances. And Miriam answered them: "Sing to the Lord, for he has triumphed gloriously! The horse and its rider he has thrown into the sea!"[7]

What a glorious picture! But it would have been more awesome if she had learned to do her praise dance on the

4. Matt 7:7a.
5. Mark 10:51.
6. Phil 4:6, 7.
7. Exod 15:20.

other side of the Red Sea. Let's impress God today. Let's thank him for things you asked for before he answers your prayer.

God always answers true prayer. God's answer can be one of three: Yes, No, or Wait! At times you may refuse to take 'No' for an answer, so it feels like God did not answer you. But he did. He said, 'No!' However, the most difficult answer to handle is 'wait.' We are living in a DSL era. We don't want to dial up and wait until it downloads. We want it now! Someone asked God for patience and prayed, "And I want it now!" Of course, God said, "Please, be patient while I am giving you patience!"

Starting with praise, confession, petition, and then thanking God in advance is the order in which you pray. If your prayer has been chaotic and random, let's put some order to it. Let's turn it into a "Cosmos Prayer."

Day 5: To Pray Like Jesus

An insight to meditate on: Respect the order in which you must pray. Praise, confession, a petition, and advance thanksgiving.

God's word to heartify: "Ask, and it will be given to you; seek, and you will find; knock, and it will be opened to you." Matt 7:7

A question to ask: Often times, rushed prayer is chaotic. How can I set a special time for prayer each day, so I can concentrate and spend planned time with God?

Let us pray: Pray according to the order of prayer you just learned. Take five minutes at each step before you go on to the next.

DAY 6: PRAYER IS PETITION—ASK, PART I

"So I say to you, ask, and it will be given to you . . ."

—LUKE 11: 9A

"The size of your God, determines the size of your prayer request. The size of your prayer request, determines the size of your answers."

—JERRY FALWELL

You do not have, because you do not *ask*.

Ask. In prayer you must learn to *ask*! At the foundational level, prayer is a petition. Basically prayer is asking God to fill all your lack and need. It is not begging. Beggers beg, but children ask!

It is true that God knows everything including all of your needs and wants, but you cannot develop an attitude that there is no need to ask anything from God because he already knows.

Jesus warned people not to be like hypocrites and to ask God in vain repetitions,[8] "For your Father knows the things you have need of before you ask him."[9] It seems from this text that you shouldn't ask God for any of your need. But this verse comes in prelude to the Lord's Prayer. In it, Jesus teaches us to make a petition for daily bread. God knows you need daily bread to survive, but he still asks you to ask him.

It is not about bread but a relationship. As you are engaged in daily communication with God, you build a dependent relationship and open communication. That is

8. Matt 6:7.

9. Matt 6:8.

what God is after. Jesus' warning about vain repetitions is repeating the same prayers ritualistically, like chanting. In such repetitions there is an empty relationship.

In Mongolia, people put their prayer list in a little metal container with a string attached to a ball. All day they will make this string go around and around, thinking that they are offering prayer to their god. In the same way, Christians can turn prayer into vain repetitions. Chanting is not communication. It is just noise.

Ask—God is good. God is our Father, and as a wonderful Father, he enjoys giving good things to his children. Of course, he wants to bless you. Jesus says it this way. "If you then, being evil, know how to give good gifts to your children, how much more will your Father who is in heaven give good things to those who ask him!"[10] Don't argue with Jesus—go ahead and ask our heavenly Father. He is good.

The benefit of loving Jesus. God especially wants to give to those who love Jesus. When you believe in Jesus and are born again, then you will become partakers of Jesus' inheritance. Jesus said to his followers, "For the Father himself loves you, because you have loved me, and have believed that I came forth from God."[11] Then he said, "Most assuredly, I say to you, whatever you ask the Father in my name he will give you. Until now you have asked nothing in my name. Ask, and you will receive, that your joy may be full."[12]

But ask for what? Wisdom. I can ask for anything? Great, what about a red Ferrari? Well, you better ask for some wisdom first. It takes wisdom to discern what you

10. Matt 7:11.
11. John 16:27.
12. John 16:23–24.

need and what is beneficial to you. If God gave me everything I asked for when I was immature, I would not be living today. At the age of 15, while riding my brother's 250cc Honda motorcycle, I sincerely felt that I needed more power and speed, and I asked God for that ultimate riding machine—the Suzuki Ninja. It rides like a bullet, and if God allowed me to have it, I wouldn't have survived to tell you about it. As a fifteen-year old, I needed more wisdom than a faster bike.

The Bible says, "If any of you lacks wisdom, let him ask of God, who gives to all liberally and without reproach, and it will be given to him."[13] Did you know that only once in the Bible is mentioned the idea of giving liberally, and it is right here. God does not mind giving all of us more wisdom. If you have little children, you can feel a bit of God's heart. "Oh, they are so immature. They need to grow up and wise up!" I think that's how our God feels. He wants to give us a lot of wisdom and then some more.

Then what? Blessing. Be wise and ask God for a blessing. But make sure you define what a blessing is for you. You see, for strawberry farmers in southern California, the definition of a blessing is a lot of rain in March. Plenty of rain in that month guarantees a great harvest. However, if you own a cherry orchard, it means disaster. Cherries are just blossoming at that time and all the flowers will be ruined. No flowers, no cherries. Can you imagine God listening to the strawberry farmer's desperate plea for rain and the cherry farmer's rebuke of the rain in Jesus' name. How does God do it? Wow . . . I am glad I am not God. But in an amazing way, he blesses all of them.

13. Jas 1:5.

What does your blessing look like? When it comes to receiving a blessing from the Lord, don't be religious and overly pietistic. Many Christians, even though they are not ready to take on the challenge, ask God to make them someone they are not ready to become. For example, many pray, "Lord, make me like Billy Graham!" God answers your prayer by sending you through hell. I mean literal hell. Sufferings will come. Trials will come. People will cheat you. People will betray you. When you are bruised black and blue, you go back to God and ask, "God I just wanted to preach the Gospel at a big stadium and see many people become Christians. I did not want any of these trials and pain?" But God sent you through all these obstacles because he was answering your prayer. You cannot achieve the character of Billy Graham's level without going through his level of suffering.

The Apostle Paul says it this way. "We also glory in tribulations, knowing that tribulation produces perseverance; and perseverance, character; and character, hope."[14] Mr. Graham had more death threats in his life time than any other leader, both in the religious and political realm, in modern day history. Can you picture this godly man on his knees before going up to the podium to preach the Gospel, after getting a death threat that the very podium he will stand on will be bombed? That was his cross! I pray that you won't ask for someone else's cross thinking that it is a blessing.

What does your blessing look like? Ask wisely!

14. Rom. 5:3.

Day 6: To Pray Like Jesus

An insight to meditate on: You have not because you ask not! Ask—but wisely.

God's word to heartify: "If you then, being evil, know how to give good gifts to your children, how much more will your Father who is in heaven give good things to those who ask him!" Matt 7:11

A question to ask: When was the last time you asked from the Lord, fully trusting that he is a good God? What does "delight yourself in the Lord" who wants to grant your heart's desire look like?[15]

Let us pray: Let's practice petitionary prayer. Let's ask God for our needs and our desires.

DAY 7: PRAYER IS PETITION—ASK, PART II

"So I say to you, ask, and it will be given to you . . . "

—LUKE 11:9A

"When people do not mind what God says to them in his word, God doth as little mind what they say to him in prayer."

—WILLIAM GURNALL

God wants to bless you—so, ask him to bless you.

But some conditions have to be met when you pray before God answers your petition. There are five conditions.

One. Ask out of a relationship. You must abide in a relationship with Christ. If a strange boy walks into my house and wants to play with my son's computer, I will say

15. Ps 37:4 "Delight yourself also in the Lord, and He shall give you the desires of your heart."

"Absolutely not!" Why? Because true petition is made in the context of relationship. Out of that relationship, you learn the desires of Christ. If you spend much time in fellowship with someone you love and respect, you will become like that person. Imagine that a brother named John worked with Mother Theresa for many years, sharing her philosophy and living by her lifestyle. A reporter comes to her ministry and interviews John, "Now that you have spent many years with Mother Theresa, what is your greatest desire?" And John replies, "All I want in life now is to get a Harley Davidson V-Rod because I have this incredible need for speed." The interview is over at this point. John never understood the heartbeat of Mother Theresa.

My fasting journey actually began when Dr. David Cho's mother-in-law, Pastor Choi Jasil, who is an incredible prayer warrior specializing in fasting, prayed for me and my wife Jenny in 1985 challenging us to fast for three days. I thank God for her and her prayer. I believe some of her fasting anointing has rubbed off on me. Praise God! To this day, I have logged more than 250 days of fasting. Have you seen a little boy in a red cape jumping off a table acting like Superman? You mimic and want to be like your hero. Because I spent time with Dr. Cho and saw how he prayed, I challenged myself to pray more and more—just like him. Jesus said, "If you abide in me, and my words abide in you, you will ask what you desire, and it shall be done for you.[16] Your desire is the by-product of an intimate relationship with God. If you spend time with Christ, then you are going to desire what he desires in the process of becoming more like him!

16. John 15:7.

Two. Ask with the right motivation. You must be motivated properly when you make a petition to the Lord. Right motivation counts—*why* you are asking counts more than *what* you are asking. The Bible says, "You ask and do not receive, because you ask amiss, that you may spend it on your pleasures."[17]

Not everything you desire is good for you. A Danish proverb notes, "Give to a pig when it grunts and a child when he cries, and you will have a fine pig and a bad child." God is raising children, not pigs. So, don't cry out for everything you want. Check your heart. Check your motives before you ask. God will provide all that you need to sustain life and enjoy what God intended for you to have. The apostle Paul said, "My God shall supply all your need according to his riches in glory by Christ Jesus." [18] Amen!

Testimony—A Ten Thousand Dollar Miracle. I had my share of experiencing God's provision according to God's glory by Christ Jesus. Many years ago, I was in an extended fast at a prayer retreat center, and the Lord told me not to be paid by my church but to live as a missionary, like Dr. Bill Bright who raised his support through individual sponsors. That was a tall order for a young pastor who was already in debt because of the ministry. But I obeyed, and God blessed me and my family tremendously. I had one objection, though. It seemed that God always answered my prayer for financial needs at the very last minute. So, one day I sought after God and honestly asked him to give me $10,000. This was my reasoning: If I opened up a savings account and linked it to my checking account, creating overdraft protec-

17. Jas 4:3.
18. Phil 4:19.

tion, then I wouldn't have to worry about my checks bouncing ever again. What a smart plan!

Shortly thereafter, I was leading a Sunday worship service in Chicago for my friend, Pastor Park. Without making an announcement beforehand, my friend decided to take a love offering for me. "That's very nice of him," I thought. Well, that night Pastor Park came over to the hotel I was staying at with the biggest wide eyes I've ever seen in an Asian man. He said, "It is a miracle! Our people gave you $9,000." The biggest offering that church had given in their entire church history was $3,000, and that was in their annual Thanksgiving offering. "Praise the Lord!" I said to my friend, but holding that check, I said to God, "But Lord, I said $10,000! Did you take the tithe already?"

Still rejoicing, I gave my wife Jenny a call with the good news. She was just finishing up with her worship service in Los Angeles due to the time difference. I said, "Jenny, the Lord gave us $9,000 out of the $10,000 we've been asking for. Praise God!" But there was a distinctive silence on the other line. "Is everything okay, honey?" I asked. What she shared with me blew me away. She said, "Well, after our worship service here, we were in the fellowship hall, and this man in a black suit (that's not normal attire in Southern California on a Sunday) came over to me and handed me a white envelope with your name on it and said, 'Give this to Pastor Oh and he will know what it is for.'" When she came home and opened it, there were ten one hundred dollar bills in it—$1,000! Wow! Praise the Lord! I have not worried about my checks bouncing ever since.

The point of my testimony is this: Honestly check your motive for asking God for money. I did not ask because I just wanted to have a lot of money in the bank. Rather, my insecurity about our finances was affecting my ministry, so I asked with a right motive and God gave me this little miracle in Chicago. To this date, the mysterious man in black never showed up again.

Three. Ask what God wants. You must ask in accordance with the will of God. Pray what he wills and he will surely answer! It's that simple. But how? Pray according to his words, all the Bible promises as your prayer requests. Let me demonstrate.

"Lord, I pray that your words be true in my life. You said that he that is in me is greater than anything that is in the world in I John 4:4. Lord, according to your word, let me be an overcomer. Don't let me blame the world for my failures, when there is a resource within me that can overcome anything that the world throws at me."

"Lord, you said in Philippians 4:13 that 'I can do all things in Christ who gives me strength!' God, give me strength to do all that I am attempting for your glory and for your kingdom's sake."

"Lord, you promised in Genesis 12 that you will make me a great nation, a great name and a source of blessing! Yes, make that a reality in my life. Lord, I want to be a source of blessing. Not only as a recipient but as a giver of your blessings out of abundance, God, pour out your blessings through me!"

"Lord, I will walk by faith and not by sight according to 2 Corinthians 5:7. Help me, O God, to see your reality, not what's out there before my eyes."

"Lord, according to Proverbs 3:5, I will not lean on my own understanding but will trust you and your words. Let me give hope to the hopeless and faith to those who are discouraged."

Do you see what I am doing? I am praying God's promises in the Bible as my prayer!

This is what the Bible says, "Now this is the confidence that we have in him, that if we ask anything according to his will, he hears us. And if we know that he hears us, whatever we ask, we know that we have the petitions that we have asked of him."[19]

Four. Ask, believing. You must ask in faith! William Gurnall said that prayer is nothing but the promise reversed and retorted by faith upon God again. That is so true. You must believe that God will answer your prayer in faith before you ask. "Without faith it is impossible to please God."[20] "And whatever things you ask in prayer, believing, you will receive."[21] If you really don't have faith for it, then don't just continue praying. You have turned prayer into vain repetition. It's nothing more than the Mongolian's tin can prayer. Stop and ask God for more and appropriate faith that will match the prayer requests. I learned this principle in a supernatural way in Florida.

Testimony. I already shared my testimony about how God told me not to be paid by the church. Well, it was April of that year. By the end of that year, although I did not take a salary from the church, God paid off all my personal debts, totaling $30,000. I have experienced miracle after miracle, but the final one was the best one.

I was preaching at a small church in Florida. I was finishing up my three days revival service on Sunday afternoon. It was the last service, and I had finished preaching, relaxing at the back of the stage while the senior pastor

19. 1 John 5:14–15.
20. Heb 11:6.
21. Matt 21:22.

was making announcements. At that moment, the Holy Spirit said to me, "I am going to take care of your credit card debt!" Just like that. Wow, I couldn't believe it. So I told God, "Lord, I cannot believe that! The meeting is over and the pastor is making the announcements." I sincerely couldn't believe that God would pay off my credit card debt at that moment. This is what God said. "Ask for faith. It is a gift of the Holy Spirit."[22] I humbled myself and asked God for faith.

At a certain point, as I was praying, I received the gift of faith. I felt the power of God come into me in the form of faith. I said to God, "Yes, Lord, I believe!" It was at that precise moment, the senior pastor of the church stopped making the announcements. He said, "Folks, I just heard from the Lord. We need to give Pastor Oh a love offering." Then he asked his elders, "Dear elders, we did not discuss this beforehand, so if you are against giving Pastor Oh a love offering, raise your hand!" Now, who in their right mind would go against such a request. The church graciously did a love offering that day.

The next day as I was getting ready to go back to Los Angeles, the pastor came over for breakfast and handed me an envelope with a check in it saying, "This includes your airfare. I am sorry; it is not too much!" It is Korean tradition to say the opposite, when you give a gift, so I knew there was quite a bit of money in that envelope. I came home and opened it, and the check was written out for $6,000. I was right—that pastor was just being polite. I subtracted my airfare and the total giving came out to be $5,560. A few days later, the bill for my credit card came with a total balance of

22. 1 Cor 12:9.

$5,550. God gave me $10 more—more than what I asked for. From that point on in my life, I ask for faith from God before I start asking from him. Ask, believing!

Five. Ask specifically. You must ask specifically so that God gets the glory afterwards.

Many times you take the credit for the good things God gives because you honestly forget that you asked for those things in the first place.

Don't ask God, "Lord, I want a good job!" What does that mean? Please do not confuse God! He wants to bless you, but your prayer at times is too vague. You see, I had been praying, "Lord, I don't want to bounce checks!" And God answered back, "OK, what do you want me to do about it? When I answer your prayer, I want you to know it was I who solved your problem." Then I answer him back, "Lord, I don't want to bounce checks!" Good grief! It goes around and around until you bounce one more check and get discouraged and say, "Oh well, God did not answer my prayer."

But when I asked for a specific amount for a specific reason, God answered me with my little miracle in Chicago with the $10,000. I will never credit myself for that. It is only God who will be exalted and glorified through that testimony. Ask specifically so he will get the credit.

Now are you ready to ask him—relationally, with a right motivation, asking what he wants and believing beforehand?

Day 7: To Pray Like Jesus

An insight to meditate on: Prayer is asking God for our specific need out of a relationship with him and having good motivation and faith.

God's word to heartify: "If you abide in me, and my words abide in you, you will ask what you desire, and it shall be done for you." John 15:7

A question to ask: Did you ask according to his will and his desires? What can I do today to ensure pure motivation for my requests to the Lord? Review and examine all of your past prayer requests and make an honest assessment.

Let us pray: Go back to your notes, and pray according to these five points: ask out of a relationship, ask with the right motivation, ask what God wants, ask believing, and ask specifically.

DAY 8: TOPICAL PRAYER[23]

"The righteous cry out, and the Lord hears, and delivers them out of all their troubles."

—Psa 34:17

"Prayer is expressing to the Lord our feelings and thoughts, with all due respect and humility, and making our requests known to the Lord, and leaving the results up to him."

—Todd Schäve

God answers prayers—keep a record!

One of the classical petitionary prayers is topical prayer. If a prayer is compared to strolling, topical prayer is

23. Cho, *How to Pray*, 26.

taking a walk with a specific destination in mind. There are five points to remember when you pray topically.

First. You must take greed out of your heart before you begin. It's a heart issue. If you make demands of God for the goals you have set with greed in your prayer, it will not be answered. You should ask the following questions: does it bring glory to God? Is my prayer in the scope of God's will for me? The Bible says that they cry out, but he does not answer, because of the pride of evil men.[24]

Your list of topics should not be random things of your desire, but an organized list of things you need to fulfill what God has in store for you. Don't ask God for a million dollars unless you are certain as to why you need such finances in your life.

Second. You must have clear-cut goals. Vague prayers are never effective. "God, we pray for your blessing!" To a prayer like that, God will respond, "But how?" If God answers that prayer, how would you know that God did, in fact, answer you? A good topical prayer has a specific goal, so you will and can testify that God answered your prayer.

> A widow comes to the judge with a plea. "Grant me justice against my adversary." Since the judge neither feared God nor cared about men, for some time he refused her. But she had a goal set before her. Until that goal was accomplished, she kept on. Finally, he said to himself, "Even though I do not fear God or care about men, yet because this widow keeps bothering me, I will see that she gets justice, so that she won't eventually wear me out with her coming!" and he granted her plea.[25]

24. Job 35:12.
25. Luke 18:1–5.

After speaking this parable, Jesus taught his disciples that God will answer our specific and persistent prayers. The Bible says that the righteous cry out, and the Lord hears, and delivers them out of all their troubles.[26] Cry out to the Lord with your topical prayers!

Third. Write out your topical prayer as a list. Keep a list in your prayer journal or inside jacket of your Bible. Carry it with you everywhere and look it up frequently. Out of sight, out of mind! I even number my prayers so that I can go back and see if God answered according to my prayer. It's really fun; try it.

Thirty-two years ago when I became a born-again Christian, I kept a few sheets of paper containing the names of people who needed to know Christ as Lord and Savior. A few hundred names were written on them. Today, that list is no more because everyone on that list became born-again Christians. Praise the Lord! I will share one fantastic testimony out of those hundreds of names I prayed for.

Testimony. I had been praying for my sister Somi for more than fifteen years. She is bright and a very successful optometrist. But she was not a Christian. As I prayed for her for those many years, I realized that she had a hard time believing in Jesus because everything in her life was going too well. So I changed my prayer strategy and started praying that she would lose everything. (Now this was many years ago and I don't pray like this anymore and don't teach as a prayer principle—Your prayer should always bless not curse.) I wrote out a prayer for her in my prayer journal with a prayer number so I could trace back. That month my sister called me. When I heard her voice, I knew she had

26. Ps 34:17.

become a born-again Christian. There was something profoundly different about her voice. Sure enough, she started telling me her testimony. This is what happened.

She said that for some reason everything was going wrong in her life. Her marriage was not doing well, and her receptionist had taken a lot of cash from her practice and fled. She was going through a major nervous breakdown. That morning as she sent her son to school and her maid home, she was taking a shower alone in her big house, when she heard the front door open. Her heart stopped. "Who could that be?" She turned off the water, but there was silence. She continued her shower. Shortly thereafter, she heard the sound of footsteps coming up to the second floor toward her bedroom. She was very scared by this time. But again, another long silence. Then she heard her bathroom door open, and without really thinking she kicked the shower door open and shouted, "Who is it?" Guess what? Right there, before her eyes, Jesus was standing. She fainted and laid in that shower stall for a few hours.

By the time she regained consciousness, she was completely dry. According to her, she had hardened her heart toward God so much that she said to herself, "Because I am going through these personal crises, I must be seeing things!" She put on her shower robe and entered her bedroom. Jesus was sitting by her bed, not speaking, but with his eyes, he said, "You still don't believe!" She collapsed on her bed this time crying out to God, "I believe, I believe. Jesus, you are real!" So, she was born-again at that moment. Praise God.

When Somi shared her testimony, I rejoiced with her. I went back to my prayer journal to see how I had prayed for her that month. This is what I had written, "Lord, I pray that you will let her stand before you naked!" And God took my prayer literally. Our God is humorous. My sister finished a two year Bible class and became a lay pastor at a wonderful church in the San Jose area.

Make an annual prayer list. Every year, our family will make a prayer goal list in January. We pray through out the year and rejoice together when God answers our prayers.

Also, when you write out a topical prayer list, make sure to be more proactive than reactive! Pray for prevention rather than intervention. Do not have a long list of crisis management type of prayer but prayers that will eliminate the crisis beforehand. For example, do more prayer on being healthy and staying healthy than healing from sickness.

Four. You should pray repeatedly and persistently. The key is to repeat the petition periodically. A topical prayer may not be answered in one day. Since it requests a specific answer, some time may pass before it is answered. Of course, praying with your heart periodically is not considered vain repetition.

Don't give up. Persist! Tenaciously hold on to the promise God gave you and persist. Jacob wrestled with an angel of God at Jabbok. He wouldn't let the angel go until he was blessed by him. God granted him his desire after that wrestling match.[27] Sometimes you need to persist and wrestle until God blesses you.

Five. You should pray patiently. When you pray for a specific topic for a while, sometimes discouragement sets in and you want to forget about the whole thing. Steadfast faith must kick in at this time.

27. Gen 32:22–26.

Testimony. I prayed for my father's salvation for about twenty years. By the time I became a born-again Christian, he left the church and joined a Japanese Buddhist cult. He also abandoned the family because that's what this cult taught him. Over the years, he became quite a prominent leader of that temple. For about seven years we did not even know where he was. Finally our family located him, living with another woman who was a part of his temple. Every time I shared the Gospel he would reject it. It displeased him greatly that his son was a Christian pastor. He took my family out of his will and gave us much pain in the process.

There was not an ounce of hope, it seemed. He closed his heart completely. After praying for him persistently and patiently—writing his name in my prayer journal and fasting and praying for him—he came to know Christ through my wife's witness three months before he went to be with the Lord. Praise God. Don't give up. Persist!

Day 8: To Pray Like Jesus

An insight to meditate on: God answers prayer—keep a record!

God's word to heartify: "The righteous cry out, and the Lord hears, and delivers them out of all their troubles." Ps 34:17

A question to ask: Have you given up on someone? Reclaim them in Jesus' name. Keep a prayer list with their names and start praying for them again. Don't give up; God will answer your sincere prayers.

Let us pray: Write out topical prayer requests now and start praying them one by one.

My Personal Topical Prayer Requests

Date	Request	Promise	Answered

DAY 9: THE RIPPLE PRAYER[28]

"You shall be witnesses to me in Jerusalem, and in all Judea and Samaria, and to the end of the earth."

—ACTS 1:8B

"I have never met a soul who has set out to satisfy the Lord and has not been satisfied himself."

—WATCHMAN NEE

Influence your world in Jesus' name!

Another classical petition prayer is called the ripple prayer. When you throw a rock into a calm lake, you will see a ripple spreading across the water. That is the basic idea of this prayer. You start at the center of the concentric circle and spread outward in sequence. It is like going from your Jerusalem, Judea, Samaria and to the end of the earth. Everyone has their scope of influence. At any level, though, you can become the influencing agent for transformation through prayer.

28. Cho, *How to Pray*, 46.

First. With myself—it begins with the nearest and spreads outward. A ripple prayer begins with yourself. It is to pray for your own life in Christ, for more of his grace and blessings, and for your various needs and problems. You should pray earnestly to God for these needs.

I am not talking about egoism or egotistic self-centeredness, but simply accepting one's self as a gift God has given to you. Fulfilling what God has called you to become is not sin.

After that is done, then you move on to the next concentric circle of your life.

Second. Pray for your immediate family. You should pray for your spouse and his or her spiritual life and health. Then you pray for your children. If you are not married, then pray for your parents or grandparents for their various needs if they are still living. Even for physical needs, the Bible teaches us to take care of our immediate family. "Let them first learn to show piety at home and to repay their parents; for this is good and acceptable before God."[29]

Third. Pray for your spiritual family. How important is your local church? It should be very important! That's your primary place of spiritual nurturing and growth. The apostle Paul encourages us to take care of our local church family first. "Therefore, as we have opportunity, let us do good to all, especially to those who are of the household of faith."[30]

Pray for your pastor. He or she needs your prayer the most because the enemy's attack is the fiercest toward them. Jesus knew that when a shepherd falls, the flock of sheep is lost. That's why Jesus said to his disciples, "All of you will be made to stumble because of me this night, for it is written: 'I will strike the Shepherd, and the sheep of the flock will be

29. 1 Tim 5:4.
30. Gal 6:10.

scattered."³¹ Pray for your pastor; your spiritual well-being depends on it.

Also, pray for your church that it will be one in unity and one purpose. The Greek word for "one accord" means "rushing together." Pray that your local church as a family of God will rush together as a river of life—giving life to everything that you touch together.

Fourth. Pray for your siblings and relatives. It is so easy to judge your own siblings and those close to you because you feel like you know them so well. That's the very reason why you need to pray for them. When you see something you dislike, do not turn it into a judgment point, but a prayer request. Jesus knew that well. That's why he said, "How can you say to your brother, 'Let me remove the speck from your eye'; and look, a plank is in your own eye?"³²

Love your brothers and sisters through prayer.

Fifth. Pray for your neighbors and friends. How would you love your neighbors? By praying for them. Keep them in your prayer list. Tell them you are praying for them. That is neighborly love you can share with them. "Pray for one another, that you may be healed."³³

Sixth. Pray for your city. Like one individual can sin, one city can sin and be punished as a corporate body. If you want concrete evidence from the Bible, just read about how God treated Sodom and Gomorrah's corporate sin. A great warning comes to us from the book of Revelation. "Babylon is fallen, is fallen, that great city, because she has made all nations drink of the wine of the wrath of her fornication."³⁴

31. Matt 26:31.
32. Matt 7:4.
33. Jas 5:16b.
34. Rev 14:8.

You need to pray for your city. There is a dominant sin of each city. You must identify it and pray against it.

Seven. Pray for America and its political leaders. Pray for the President and ask God's wisdom to be with him. How do you lead a country without God's guidance? Listen to what the apostle Paul says to the Christians who lived in Rome, which was the leading country of his time. "Let every soul be subject to the governing authorities. For there is no authority except from God, and the authorities that exist are appointed by God. Therefore whoever resists the authority resists the ordinance of God, and those who resist will bring judgment on themselves."[35]

Eight. Pray for other countries. Finally, you pray for all the people in other countries. God will put a special country on your heart. Be a nation taker—at least in your prayer. Find out all about that country and pray with knowledge and understanding.

For example, if you are praying for Cambodia, you should know something about her political structure and immediate needs. For effective prayer, you should keep a sheet handy with all the needed information.[36]

Learning different ways to pray is like acquiring different techniques of painting using different kinds of material. Ultimately, a picture is drawn. Sometimes with oil and other times with pastel. A real artist can use many modes of drawing to create beautiful art work. In the same way, it is with a seasoned prayer warrior. You should be able to pray different prayers according to the different situations and specific spiritual climates and needs. Prayer is an art!

35. Rom 13:1–2.

36. Johnstone and Mandryk, *Operation World: 21st Century Edition.* This book lists all the vital information on each country.

Try the different types of prayer each day that you have learned so far.

Day 9: To Pray Like Jesus

An insight to meditate on: Influence your world through prayer!

God's word to heartify: "You shall be witnesses to me in Jerusalem, and in all Judea and Samaria, and to the end of the earth." Acts 1:8b

A question to ask: What is my circle of influence? What must I do to go to the next level of influence? Have I been too selfish and prayed only for those immediately around me?

Let us pray: Pray through your concentric circles. Write out a prayer list at each level.

- Myself:
- Family:
- Spiritual Family:
- Siblings/Relatives:
- Neighbors/Friends:
- City:
- Nations/Political leaders:
- World:

DAY 10: PRAYER IS DEVOTION—SEEK

"Seek, and you will find . . ."

—LUKE 11:9B

*"There is nothing that makes us love a person
so much as prayer for them."*

—WILLIAM LAW

Seek God, and you will find him.

From 'What' to 'Whom.' So far you have learned about the petitionary prayer which is very important prayer. But there is more to prayer than that. We are going to switch from the 'what' of petitionary prayer to the 'whom' of devotional prayer.

You will find a great example of such a prayer in the life of Moses. Moses warns the Israelites that God will scatter them if they do not obey God's words. "But from there you will seek the Lord your God, and you will find him if you seek him with all your heart and with all your soul."[37] What Moses describes here is the picture of our next prayer level. It's called seeking prayer or devotional prayer.

God's Treasure. God wants to bring us into such close communion with him because he wants to share his most intimate treasure of wisdom and knowledge with you. The Bible says, "The secret things belong to the Lord our God, but those things which are revealed belong to us and to our children forever, that we may do all the words of this law."[38] But it takes effort to get the treasures that God desires to give us.

It takes diligence. The writer of Proverbs says it plainly. "I love those who love me, and those who seek me diligently will find me. Riches and honor are with me, enduring riches and righteousness. My fruit is better than gold, yes, than fine gold, and my revenue than choice silver."[39]

The writer of Hebrews also has the same challenge, "For God is not unjust to forget your work and labor of love

37. Deut 4:29.
38. Deut 29:29.
39. Prov 8:17–19.

which you have shown toward his name, in that you have ministered to the saints, and do minister. And we desire that each one of you show the same diligence to the full assurance of hope until the end, that you do not become sluggish, but imitate those who through faith and patience inherit the promise."[40]

The sluggish Christian is not willing to seek, so he will never enter into the fullness of the blessing that God has desired him to have. The Bible says, "Hear instruction and be wise, and do not disdain it. Blessed is the man who listens to me, watching daily at my gates, waiting at the posts of my doors. For whoever finds me finds life, and obtains favor from the Lord."[41] It takes discipline and effort to live your life at the doorpost of the Lord. But the reward is great!

Seek him. At the core of devotional prayer is God. In a nutshell, it is turning your petitionary prayer such as, "Lord I need money!" to devotional prayer such as, "Lord, you are my provider!" It may sound like the same thing, but it isn't. The former is seeking the goods; the latter is seeking the giver.

When you are seeking God, make sure you do not conjure up images that are not biblical images of God. Always go back to the Bible and base your seeking from the Word of God. There are seven Hebrew names of God, representing his character that you can seek after.

The seven Hebrew names of God—declare who God is! When God said to Moses, "I am that I am,"[42] he means that "He is the becoming one." He will become the God who can help you with your need in the current situation. Our God

40. Heb 6:10–12.
41. Prov 8:33–35.
42. Exod 3:14.

has many names to become the one you are in desperate need for.

1. He is Jehovah-Jireh. It means, "the Lord will provide." When Abraham offered his son Isaac on the mountain of Moriah in obedience to God's command, God stopped him and provided a ram instead. So Abraham offered the ram as a burnt offering and called the name of that place Jehovah-Jireh.[43] Through this name, God shows that he provides for all of us.

Are you in need of something? Go ahead, call his name, Jehovah-Jirah, and pray unto the Lord. He will provide all of your needs and wants.

2. He is Jehovah-Rophe. God says to the people of Israel that he is the Lord who heals them.[44] The God of the Old Testament is the healer. In the same way, our Lord Jesus took our infirmities on his body in obedience to the will of his Father. The Bible says that Jesus "bore our sins in his own body on the tree, that we, having died to sins, might live for righteousness—by whose stripes you were healed."[45] Our God is the healer. Go ahead and pray, "Jehovah-Rophe, you can heal my body, emotions, and relationships!"

3. He is Jehovah-Nissi. It means, "The Lord is my banner."[46] You are, in fact, praying, "You are my victory in all conflicts and all of my life's confrontations!" Israel was attacked by the Amalekites when they arrived in Rephidim. Moses sent Joshua with the soldiers to the battlefield, but he took Aaron and Hur to the top of a hill to pray together.

43. Gen 22:14.
44. Exod 15:26.
45. 1 Pet 2:24.
46. Exod 17:15.

By having Moses' arms up until the going down of the sun, Joshua and the Israelites defeated the Amalekites. There Moses built an altar and called it "Jehovah-Nissi." What conflicts are you struggling with right now? Declare his name into your situation. Lift up your arms in prayer and call his name, Jehovah-Nissi. He will make you victorious over all of your struggles.

4. *Jehovah-Shammah*. "God is present with me." It means that God's presence will always be in his temple throughout the millennium. [47] God, you are here! I am never alone! What a wonderful confession to our Lord Jesus who has promised us that he will never leave us but will be with us until the end of all ages.[48] Hallelujah!

5. *Jehovah-Rohi*. "God is my shepherd."[49] God, you lead me and feed me and protect me! God reveals himself to us as our shepherd through the Bible. He leads, feeds and protects us as a true shepherd. You should put your trust in him and declare, "Jesus, my Lord, you are my shepherd. I shall not be in want." Turn that declaration into a confession. He will come and lead you in an intimate way—like a loving shepherd leads his sheep.

6. *Jehovah-Tsidkenu*. "God is my righteousness." God, you accept me and forgive me because of Jesus! The Bibles says, "In his days Judah will be saved and Israel will live in safety. This is the name by which he will be called: the Lord

47. Ezek 48:35.

48. Matt 1:23 "Behold, a virgin shall be with child, and shall bring forth a son, and they shall call his name Emmanuel, which being interpreted is, God with us."

49. Ps 23:1.

our righteousness."[50] God took Jesus who was sinless and willed him to become sin in your place so you might have the righteousness through him.

7. Jehovah-Shalom. "God is my peace."[51] God, you give me peace in spite of the circumstances! When Gideon saw God, he became terrified and thought he would die because no sinner would survive after seeing God.[52] But God assures him that he will not die. There Gideon built an altar unto the Lord and called it "Jehovah-Shalom."

Think on the implications of these names, and you'll have plenty to pray and praise God for! God will make special covenants with you by his names, and he will perform the work that his names imply. Go ahead and apply the names of God to situations that you are in and activate the power of his names over your problems.

Day 10: To Pray Like Jesus

An insight to meditate on: Seek God, and you will find him.

God's word to heartify: "I love those who love me, and those who seek me diligently will find me." Prov 8:17

A question to ask: Is your prayer more than just asking? Do you seek the relationship with the Lord in your prayer?

Let us pray: Let's try to pray this seeking prayer.

50. Jer 23:6.
51. Judg 6:24.
52. Exod 33:20.

God's Name	Your Prayer Requests
Jehovah-Jireh "God is my Provider"	1. 2. 3.
Jehovah-Rophe "God is my Healer"	1. 2. 3.
Jehovah-Nissi "God is my Banner"	1. 2. 3.
Jehovah-Shammah "God is Present with me"	1. 2. 3.
Jehovah-Rohi "God is my Shepherd"	1. 2. 3.
Jehovah-Tsidkenu "God is my Righteousness"	1. 2. 3.
Jehovah-Shalom "God is my Peace"	1. 2. 3.

DAY 11: PRAYER CONQUERS OVER YOUR FLESH AND MIND

"Do not be conformed to this world, but be transformed by the renewing of your mind, that you may prove what is that good and acceptable and perfect will of God."

—ROM 12:2

"Lord, although I am sure of my position, without your help I cannot maintain it. Help me or I am lost!"

—Martin Luther

You can overcome your flesh.

When you study the word, your faith is increased. The Bible says that faith comes by hearing God's words.[53] But when you pray, you are putting on the power of God. Prayer gives you power.

How do you overcome your own fleshly desires and the deception of your mind? You cannot spend the rest of your life fighting the same battles over and over again. You must put on the character of God and overcome it at some point. God's character becomes the power to overcome your flesh and its sinful passion. "For when we were in the flesh, the sinful passions which were aroused by the law were at work in our members to bear fruit to death."[54]

Dr. Cho writes, "Prayer breaks your ego and stubbornness. Living out the Christian life is not pulling God down to you but humbling yourself so that you may draw nigh to the infinite God. Prayer leads us to God. Then we can live God-centered lives."[55]

First. You must be led by the Holy Spirit. When you are seeking him in prayer, God will lead you supernaturally. The apostle Paul says that there is an incredible freedom in following God. "If you are led by the Spirit, you are not under the law."[56]

53. Rom 10:17.
54. Rom 7:5.
55. Cho, *Born to be Blessed*, 133.
56. Gal 5:18.

You have to recognize the fact that God wants to lead you. He is your shepherd. He was the pillar of cloud and the pillar of fire that led the Israelites in the desert. Jesus told his disciples to follow him. In the same way, the Holy Spirit wants to lead you, but you must give him your absolute trust and obedience.

Testimony. Many years ago, I was driving home from a long day of ministry. An early morning Bible study for businessmen at 6:00 am in downtown Los Angeles, then a preaching session at a university in the evening at a different city, and finally, a leadership training for my church in another city which ended around 11:00 pm. I was exhausted. I was so glad that I was going home. Then the Holy Spirit spoke to me. "I want you to go see Jay right now!"[57] I thought to myself, "God, have I not done enough for you today?" But, of course, I cannot say that to God. So I started making excuses. "Lord, first of all, I don't know his address. And secondly, I don't have his phone number." I had a rock solid case against his request. I was happy that I was going home. The Holy Spirit spoke to me again. "I will lead you there!" By this time, I thought to myself, "OK, I have finally entered into the Twilight Zone! This is too weird. This can't be God. But I know his voice. It is him! The sheep hears the voice of the shepherd!"

I took a deep breath and took the longest leap of faith that night. I told the Holy Spirit, "Go ahead. You are on!" The Holy Spirit started directing me. He told me to get off the freeway and take a local street. Then he told me to get on a different freeway. He told me to exit at a certain street. Make a left turn. Make a right turn. Then he told me to park my car

57. Not his real name.

and look to the left. When I did, my heart absolutely stopped. There he was, Jay, mopping the floor of a sandwich shop. I was able to see him through the window. It was around 11:45 pm. I knocked on the door and he came out. Now he looked like his heart stopped. "How did you know I was working here?" "Hmm, a very interesting question," I thought, "because I didn't even know he worked at all!" "Well, God led me here! Is there any reason why I need to see you?" Jay broke down on the floor and wept. This is his story.

Jay's father abandoned the family six months ago, causing a great financial burden. He was going to college at the time but had to work at two different places to help out with the family. He said that after that sandwich shop, he would have to go to another place to work. Literally, the only time anybody could see him was between 11:30 to 12:30 am when he was closing down the shop. Then he said, "I was so ashamed about what happened that I couldn't share it with anybody. I have been asking God to send you to me for the last six months, Pastor Oh, so I can share this burden and ask you for prayer!" I broke down and wept as I was praying for him. God knows what he is doing. He led me to a brother who needed God's assurance that he cared for him. Thank you, Lord.

The next morning I took out the map of Southern California and found out that the Holy Spirit had led me through two different cities to get me to Jay's place the night before. Isn't our God incredible?

Can the Holy Spirit lead? Yes, absolutely! I would give him my steering wheel any time of the day.

Second. Your mind has to be in sync with your prayer. Prayer is the power in which your thoughts and desires become reality. "Do not be conformed to this world, but be transformed by the renewing of your mind, that you may prove what is that good and acceptable and perfect will of God."[58]

Do not think with your mind and decide beforehand what needs to be done, but ask God to join in your work at the beginning stage. First, pray and humbly ask God what should be the order in which his work can be accomplished through you. Your mind should not control your prayer, but the other way around.

Third. Your mind has to be controlled by the Word of God. Someone said that you cannot be so spiritual that you become un-Scriptural. How true! Sometimes, your mind can speak to you in many different voices. You must discern from the Word of God and biblical principles. Jesus heard Satan's sweet voice to turn rock into bread. Actually, as I am writing this I am on my thirty-seventh day of fasting. Hmm . . . bread! That sounds great. The only problem is that I cannot turn rock into bread. But our Lord Jesus was more than able. Yet, Jesus answered him, saying, "It is written, 'Man shall not live by bread alone, but by every word of God.'"[59]

The Word of God becomes the measuring stick of what is allowed and what isn't. When you are in doubt, turn to the Word of God. "For the word of God is living and powerful, and sharper than any two-edged sword, piercing even to the division of soul and spirit, and of joints and marrow, and is a discerner of the thoughts and intents of the heart."[60]

Dr. Robert Schuller's Testimony. Dr. Schuller wrote, "I am personally indebted to Paul Yonggi Cho for spiritual

58. Rom. 12:2.
59. Luke 4:4.
60. Heb 4:12.

strength and for insights I have received from God through this great pastor."[61] He tells his story in his autobiography.

While ministering in Korea at Dr. Cho's church, Dr. Schuller heard the news of his daughter's near-fatal motorcycle accident. He writes about that event as follows:

> Dr. Cho and his wife Grace and we held our hands together. "Let's pray," Cho said. Our wet eyes closed. And I heard these godly, positive Pentecostal murmurings over and over, "Alleluia." "Alleluia." "Alleluia." I had entered another room in the mansion of prayer in which my soul had never been before in its adventure with God! Call the room "Prayers of Praise and Thanksgiving." Call it the "Allelujah" room . . . Then and there my soul was lifted. For the first time in my life I discovered the peace and the power in praise."[62]

What Dr. Schuller experienced that day is a prayer that conquers over our flesh and mind. It was a prayer led by the Holy Spirit, going beyond human reason and common sense. It was a supernatural prayer that brought about supernatural results.

No wonder God wants us to pray! Are you excited? Come on, let's pray like never before!

61. Kennedy, *Dream Your Way to Success: The Story of Dr. Yonggi Cho and Korea*, cover quotation.

62. Schuller and Cho, *Expand Your Horizon: How to Make Your Faith Work!*, 171–172.

Day 11: To Pray Like Jesus

An insight to meditate on: You can overcome your flesh.

God's word to heartify: "And do not be conformed to this world, but be transformed by the renewing of your mind, that you may prove what is that good and acceptable and perfect will of God." Rom 12:2

A question to ask: Do you let the Holy Spirit lead you in your prayer? What can you do today to overcome your fleshly passion and deception of mind?

Let us pray: Let's pray and ask the Holy Spirit to lead and guide us. Are there any issues in your life that needs solid leading? Write them down, and let's go to him in prayer.

DAY 12: TABERNACLE PRAYER, PART I

"Jesus Christ himself being the chief cornerstone,
in whom the whole building, being fitted together,
grows into a holy temple in the Lord . . ."

—EPH 2:20B–21

"We are at this moment as close to God as we really choose to be. True, there are times when we would like to know a deeper intimacy, but when it comes to the point, we are not prepared to pay the price involved."

—J. OSWALD SANDERS

You are God's temple!

A tabernacle prayer affirms and deepens your relationship with Christ. God showed Moses how to build the tabernacle according to the divine plan. The Israelites came and worshiped God there. The tabernacle is a model that teaches us the proper process of worship.[63]

The Bible says, "you are God's temple."[64] When you pray the Tabernacle Prayer, you will take the steps in which the tabernacle was built: seven categories of prayer is in connection with the seven installations of the tabernacle.

The tabernacle has two major parts, the sanctuary and the courtyard. The sanctuary was divided into two parts by a curtain, the Holy Place and the Most Holy Place. There was an altar and a basin in the courtyard; a lampstand, a show-bread table, and an altar of incense in the Holy Place; and the ark of the covenant in the Most Holy Place. The cover of the ark is called the atonement cover or the Mercy Seat.

Prayer in the Courtyard

Prayer at the Bronze Altar. In the tabernacle, the first place you arrive at is the bronze altar.[65] The altar signifies God's judgment. Since all men are sinners, all are under God's judgment.[66] You cannot go beyond that point without dealing with the basic problem of sin. For this reason, the Israelites brought an animal sacrifice to him. By shedding their blood, the Israelites transferred their sin to the sacrifice. Its blood was poured out, and its flesh burnt at the altar.

This represents the cross of Calvary where Jesus Christ became a sacrifice for us. Although he was without sin,

63. For more information, see www.domini.org/tabern/tabhome.htm

64. 1 Cor 3:16.

65. Exod 27:1–8.

66. Rom 5:8.

he became the sacrifice for us. John the Baptist shouted, "Behold! The Lamb of God who takes away the sin of the world!"[67] Jesus died for you that you may live. Praise the Lord! At this place you need to offer the following seven thanksgiving prayers. The Bible challenges you to continue earnestly in prayer, being vigilant in it with thanksgiving.[68]

First. Thank and praise Jesus for washing your sin and saving you. Jesus according to his mercy saved you, through the washing of regeneration and renewing of the Holy Spirit.[69] Invite the Holy Spirit to help you with this prayer of thanksgiving.

Second. Thank him for his deliverance from God's judgment. Jesus delivered you from the eternal judgment through his sacrifice on the cross. Jesus came to proclaim liberty to the captives and to set at liberty those who are oppressed.[70]

Third. Thank him for reconciling you with God and granting you the right to come to God. Because of what Jesus did and by the work of the precious blood, you can now approach God directly. The veil, which represents the body of Christ, separating the Most Holy Place from the Holy Place split open as Jesus breathed his last. "Then, behold, the veil of the temple was torn in two from top to bottom; and the earth quaked."[71] You have free access to God because of what Jesus did on the cross. Now, can you thank God for that in your own words?

67. John 1:29.
68. Col 4:2.
69. Titus 3:5.
70. Luke 4:18.
71. Matt. 27:51.

Fourth. Thank him for defeating the power and the authority of the devil. The Bible says that Christians overcome the enemy "by the blood of the Lamb and by the word of their testimony."[72] Indeed Satan is disarmed and his power destroyed by the power of Jesus' blood. Thank Jesus for that in your own words.

Fifth. Thank God for healing and good health through the blood of Jesus Christ. The Bible says, "by his wounds we are healed."[73] You should declare health through the wounds of Jesus and thank him in your own words.

Sixth. Thank God for delivering you from all the curses of the enemy through Jesus' blood. "Christ redeemed us from the curse of the law by becoming a curse for us, for it is written: 'Cursed is everyone who is hung on a tree.'"[74] Pray in your own words a thanksgiving to God for such incredible favor.

Seventh. Thank God for delivering you from death. Through the resurrection of Jesus Christ, you have been moved from death to eternal life. At the bronze altar, under the cross of Christ, praise Jesus for his precious blood, which was shed for you. You should start your daily Christian life from under the cross.

Prayer at the Basin.

The basin represents sanctification.[75] Here, the priests would wash themselves and be cleansed before entering the

72. Rev 12:11.
73. Isa 53:5.
74. Gal 3:13.
75. Exod 30:17–21.

sanctuary. The prayers you say here are prayers for cleansing and sanctification.

First. Pray, "Father, please make me righteous. I cannot be righteous by my own strength; it is only you who can sanctify me! Please forgive me for my unrighteous thoughts and judgments."

Second. Pray, "Father, make me honest." The first crisis of the church was lying and deception. The apostle Peter said to the offender, "Ananias, why has Satan filled your heart to lie to the Holy Spirit and keep back part of the price of the land for yourself?"[76] Selling his land and giving it to the church was a noble act, but lying about the amount was not acceptable. Ananias died because of this sin. Talking about the devil, Jesus said, "When he speaks a lie, he speaks from his own resources, for he is a liar and the father of it."[77] As you start the day, ask the Lord to cleanse you from deceptions and lies.

Third. Pray, "Father, make me faithful in every area of my life." It is required that those who have been given a trust prove faithful.[78] The Bible teaches that as Christians, we ought to engage in our work "not with eye service, as men-pleasers, but as bondservants of Christ, doing the will of God from the heart, with good will doing service, as to the Lord, and not to men."[79]

Pray that you will be faithful to the work God has given you to do today.

76. Acts 5:3.
77. John 8:44.
78. 1 Cor 4:2.
79. Eph 6:6–7.

Fourth. Pray, "Father, make me pure and holy." Christians must lead a holy life. But it is neither automatic nor easy. Without relying on God, it is impossible. So you pray, "God, sanctify my acts and words so that I will live a pure and holy life."

Jesus said, "Blessed are the pure in heart, for they shall see God."[80] And the apostle Paul warns us to, "Flee also youthful lusts; but pursue righteousness, faith, love, peace with those who call on the Lord out of a pure heart."[81] Pray for purity and holiness; then go and live a pure and holy life.

Fifth. Pray, "Father, give me the power to forgive and love." It is extremely important to forgive all people. Jesus commanded people to forgive one another whenever they pray.

If you do not forgive, the Bible says that you will not be forgiven. "For if you forgive men their trespasses, your heavenly Father will also forgive you. But if you do not forgive men their trespasses, neither will your Father forgive your trespasses."[82]

On the cross our Lord Jesus said, "Father, forgive them, for they do not know what they do."[83] Fix your eyes on Jesus on that cross and pray to forgive all who have sinned against you.

Sixth. Pray, "Father, make me meek and humble." Unless you are meek and humble, you are likely to become proud and that's where the downhill journey begins. God hates pride. C. S. Lewis said that, "Pride is a spiritual cancer." With pride comes destruction. This is why you need

80. Matt 5:8.
81. 2 Tim 2:22.
82. Matt 6:14–15.
83. Luke 23:34.

to ask God for humility. There are two options. Either you humble yourself before God or he will humble you. Take the first option, or else you will be fighting God. "God resists the proud, but gives grace to the humble."[84]

Seventh. Pray, "Father, do not let me covet." The Bible says that greed is idolatry. "Therefore put to death your members which are on the earth: fornication, uncleanness, passion, evil desire, and covetousness, which is idolatry."[85] Pray to God that you will not commit the sin of idolatry.

Day 12: To Pray Like Jesus

An insight to meditate on: You are God's temple!

God's word to heartify: "Christ has redeemed us from the curse of the law, having become a curse for us." Gal 3:13a

A question to ask: What can you do today to purify yourself? Is there anyone in your life you have not forgiven?

Let us pray: Let's pray through the first steps of the Tabernacle Prayer.

Item	Today in Prayer	Your Prayer
Bronze Altar	Pray the prayer of Thanksgiving.	1. 2. 3.
Basin	The prayer of Purification is offered through repentance.	1. 2. 3.

84. Jas 4:6b.
85. Col 3:5.

DAY 13: TABERNACLE PRAYER, PART II: PRAYER IN THE HOLY PLACE

*"Do you not know that you are the temple of God
and that the Spirit of God dwells in you?"*

—1 Cor 3:16

*"The whole purpose for which we exist is to be taken into the
life of God."*

—C.S. Lewis

The Spirit of God dwells in you!

Prayer at the Lampstand.

After cleansing yourself at the basin, you can now enter the sanctuary. In the holy place, there is a lampstand made of pure gold.[86] The lampstand has seven branches, which indicates the seven spirits of the Lord.[87] There is no other light than the lampstand, which symbolizes the Holy Spirit. He is the only light that illuminates the will of God. It takes much prayer and the fullness of his Spirit to receive the illumination and the revelation of the Spirit.

You need to say the following seven prayers to the Holy Spirit.

First. The Holy Spirit is the Spirit of God and he dwells in you. "Do you not know that you are the temple of God and that the Spirit of God dwells in you?"[88] So you should pray that the Spirit of God will be increased within you with his glory.

86. Exod 25:31–34.
87. Rev 1:4.
88. 1 Cor 3:16.

Second. The Holy Spirit is the Spirit of wisdom. So you should pray, "Spirit of wisdom, give me the wisdom to solve all the problems." The Bible says that wisdom is something that he wants to give liberally. "If any of you lacks wisdom, let him ask of God, who gives to all liberally and without reproach, and it will be given to him.[89]

Third. The Holy Spirit is the Spirit of understanding. So you should pray, "Spirit of understanding, please make me understand everything that's happening in my life and your will for my life." The Bible challenges us not to be unwise, but understand what the will of the Lord is.[90]

Fourth. The Holy Spirit is the Spirit of counsel. So you should pray, "Spirit of counsel, give me the power to counsel and guide people to your ways." As God's children, the Bible says that you are led by the Spirit of God.[91] You can guide others because you are following the leadership of the Holy Spirit.

Fifth. The Holy Spirit is the Spirit of power. So you should pray, "Spirit of power, make me a powerful Christian." Jesus gave his disciples 'power.' When Jesus had called his twelve disciples to him, "He gave them power over unclean spirits, to cast them out, and to heal all kinds of sickness and all kinds of disease."[92]

Sixth. The Holy Spirit is the Spirit of the knowledge of God. So you should pray, "Spirit of knowledge, reveal the deep truths of God to me." The apostle Paul prays for the Colossians that they may be "filled with the knowledge

89. Jas 1:5.
90. Eph 5:17.
91. Rom 8:14.
92. Matt 10:1.

of his will in all wisdom and spiritual understanding; that they may walk worthy of the Lord, fully pleasing him, being fruitful in every good work and increasing in the knowledge of God."[93]

Seven. The Holy Spirit is the Spirit of worship. So you should pray, "Spirit of worship, help me to worship God and him only with prayers and praises fervently." The Bible warns his people not to worship other gods, for the Lord, whose name is Jealous, is a jealous God.[94] "And if you by any means forget the Lord your God, and follow other gods, and serve them and worship them, I testify against you this day that you shall surely perish."[95] Ask the Holy Spirit to lead you to the true worship of God today.

Prayer at the Showbread Table.

On the right hand side of the sanctuary, there is the table of showbread.[96] The showbread was always there to represent the Word of God. The showbread receives light from the lampstand. Without the light the bread would be no longer visible. Therefore, you have to thank God for the Holy Spirit to illumine the Word of God applicable to you.

In front of the showbread table you pray the following seven prayers of God's word fervently.

First. Pray, "Let me love your word." When you love the Word of God, you are, in fact, loving our Lord Jesus. The Bible teaches that, "In the beginning was the Word, and

93. Col 1:9–10.
94. Exod 34:14.
95. Deut 8:19.
96. Exod 25:23–30.

the Word was with God, and the Word was God. And the Word became flesh and dwelt among us, and we beheld his glory, the glory as of the only begotten of the Father, full of grace and truth."[97] Jesus is that Word which became flesh. Jesus himself said, "He who does not love me does not keep my words; and the word which you hear is not mine but the Father's who sent me."[98] Go ahead, jump into his word and fall in love with Jesus.

Second. Pray, "Let me read and understand your word." Are you just reading the word or do you understand what you are reading? The key is to 'listen' to his word. Jesus said, "Why do you not understand my speech? Because you are not able to listen to my word."[99] Pray that you will open your heart to his word and listen. Pray for God's revelation through his words today.

Third. Pray, "Let me believe your word." Understanding and believing is two different things. I can understand medically and physically that my body is able to run a full marathon, but to actually believe you can run it is different. When I ran my marathon, it was not because I understood the concept, but because I believed. Jesus said, "Most assuredly, I say to you, he who hears my word and believes in him who sent me has everlasting life, and shall not come into judgment, but has passed from death into life.[100] You cannot just understand that Jesus is Savior; you must believe in him.

So pray that you will believe in God's word!

97. John 1:1, 14.
98. John 14:24.
99. John 8:43.
100. John 5:24.

Fourth. Pray, "Let me meditate and heartify your word." The Bible says that the righteous man delights in the law of the Lord, and in his law he meditates day and night.[101] Once there is understanding and you believe, then go to the next level and make it really yours. It is like the word becoming flesh in you. It can become so a part of you that the word becomes alive through your life.

Fifth. Pray, "Let me apply your word." Out of meditation and obedience comes action. Doing the word is critical in your Christian life. Jesus defines his primary relationships with ones who obey his words. Jesus responded to those who were asking about his family, "My mother and my brothers are these who hear the word of God and do it."[102] Then he went on saying, "More than that, blessed are those who hear the word of God and keep it!"[103] Pray that you can apply God's word today.

Sixth. Pray, "Let me appreciate and be nourished by your word." Have your quiet time daily like eating breakfast. Don't skip breakfast; it's not good for your health. Don't skip your quiet time; it's not good for your spiritual health. Jesus responded to Satan's temptation saying, "It is written, 'Man shall not live by bread alone, but by every word of God.'"[104] God's word is that important. Pray that you will faithfully and fervently consume God's word each day.

Seventh. Pray, "Let me share, teach and demonstrate your word." Jesus taught us to share God's word by demonstration. He constantly spoke the word to them as they

101. Ps 1:2.
102. Luke 8:21.
103. Luke 11:28.
104. Luke 4:4.

were able to hear it.[105] And Jesus empowered his disciples to go out and preach everywhere and confirmed their word through accompanying signs.[106] When Christians of the First century went out and started sharing God's word, the Bible says that the word of God grew and multiplied.[107] What a beautiful picture! Pray that you can be a part of that word, growing and multiplying in your circle of influence.

Let's invite the presence of the Holy Spirit and honor the Word of God.

Day 13: To Pray Like Jesus

An insight to meditate on: The Spirit of God dwells in you!

God's word to heartify: "Do you not know that you are the temple of God and that the Spirit of God dwells in you?" 1 Cor 3:16

A question to ask: Who is the Holy Spirit to you? Let's welcome him into our lives.

Let us pray:

Item	Today in Prayer	Your Prayer
Lampstand	The seven spirits of the Holy Spirit (Rev. 1:4)	1. 2. 3.
Showbread Table	Pray to be able to stand on his word.	1. 2. 3.

---

105. Mark 4:33.
106. Mark 16:20.
107. Acts 12:24.

DAY 14: TABERNACLE PRAYER, PART III: PRAYER IN THE MOST HOLY PLACE

"Beloved, I pray that you may prosper in all things and be in health, just as your soul prospers."

—3 John 2

"O Lord, remember not only the men and women of good will, but also those of ill will. But do not remember all of the sufferings they have inflicted upon us."

—A prayer found
at Ravensbruck Concentration Camp

You will prosper in all things!

Prayer at the Incense Altar.

The altar of incense lies between the lampstand and the showbread table.[108] There, priests burned incense twenty-four hours a day. This represents our constant praise before God. The incense is visible only when there is light in the room. Once again, the Holy Spirit and his light is needed to inspire true praises to God. At the incense altar you can pray the following seven prayers of praise. You can freely sing praises unto the Lord. Remember that your praise is a harmonized prayer. Do not rush through but spend ample time soaking in God's presence through your private praise and worship.

First. Praise God for saving you from sin. Recite these Psalms and praise God for the salvation you have received. "My soul shall be joyful in the Lord; It shall rejoice in his

108. Exod 30:1–10.

salvation.[109] "We will rejoice in your salvation, and in the name of our God we will set up our banners!"[110] "The Lord lives! Blessed be my Rock! Let the God of my salvation be exalted."[111]

Second. Praise God for filling you with the Spirit. The Bible says that the disciples were filled with joy and with the Holy Spirit.[112] In the same way, you may be filled with all the fullness of God.[113] So, "Do not be drunk with wine, in which is dissipation; but be filled with the Spirit."[114] Praise God that he wants to fill us with his Spirit.

Third. Praise God for healing you. God's Spirit was upon Jesus and anointed him to heal the brokenhearted, and recover sight to the blind.[115] The same Spirit of God wants to heal your broken heart and give you spiritual insights to life. Praise God for that healing and receive it in faith.

Fourth. Praise God for giving you the blessing of Abraham. "Therefore know that only those who are of faith are sons of Abraham. And the Scripture, foreseeing that God would justify the Gentiles by faith, preached the gospel to Abraham beforehand, saying, 'In you all the nations shall be blessed.' So then those who are of faith are blessed with believing Abraham."[116] What an incredible blessing! Praise God for that.

109. Ps 35:9.
110. Ps 20:5.
111. Ps 18:46.
112. Acts 13:52.
113. Eph 3:19.
114. Eph 5:18.
115. Luke 4:18.
116. Gal 3:6–9.

Fifth. Praise God for delivering you from temptation and trials. The Bible says, "No temptation has overtaken you except such as is common to man; but God is faithful, who will not allow you to be tempted beyond what you are able, but with the temptation will also make the way of escape, that you may be able to bear it.[117]

Sixth. Praise God for turning a curse into a blessing for you. "Christ has redeemed us from the curse of the law, having become a curse for us."[118] And you can praise God in advance for the kingdom of God you will enter. "There shall be no more curse, but the throne of God and of the Lamb shall be in it, and his servants shall serve him."[119]

Seventh. Praise God for making you the representative of Christ on earth. Paul and Barnabas boldly proclaimed that the Lord has commanded: "I have set you as a light to the Gentiles, that you should be for salvation to the ends of the earth.'"[120] As Christians, we are light to the world—we are representatives of Christ on earth. Praise God for that privilege.

Prayer at the Ark of the Covenant

There is the Ark of the Covenant in the middle of the Most High Place.[121] The Ark was made of acacia wood and covered with pure gold. Inside the Ark, there were the stone

117. 1 Cor 10:13.
118. Gal 3:13a.
119. Rev 22:3.
120. Acts 13:46–47.
121. Exod 25:10–16.

tablets of the covenant, a jar of manna, and Aaron's staff that had budded.

The Ark represents Jesus our Lord; the tablets signify Jesus as the Word; the jar of manna signifies him as the bread of life; and the budded staff signifies him as the life of resurrection. So in front of the Ark, which represents Christ, you should make the following seven confessions.

First. Confess, "Jesus, you are the new covenant of my salvation." The writer of Hebrews tells us that because of this new covenant, Jesus will put his words in your heart and write them in your mind.[122] Confess Jesus as your salvation.

Second. Confess, "Jesus, you are the new manna, the bread of my life." Jesus said, "I am the bread of life. He who comes to me shall never hunger, and he who believes in me shall never thirst."[123] Confess him to be the bread of life in your own words.

Third. Confess, "Jesus, you are my only hope of resurrection." Jesus said, "I am the resurrection and the life. He who believes in me, though he may die, he shall live."[124] Recognize that and confess him to be your only hope of resurrection.

Fourth. Confess, "Jesus, you are my joy and my strength."

Jesus promised that his "joy may remain in you, and that your joy may be full."[125] King David confessed that in a song when God delivered him from the hand of Saul, "God

122. Heb 10:16.
123. John 6:35.
124. John 11:25.
125. John 15:11.

is my strength and power, and he makes my way perfect.[126] Confess that in your own life. Let the joy and the strength of God be yours today.

Fifth. Confess, "Jesus, you are my righteousness." Now this is his name by which he will be called: The Lord our Righteousness.[127] The apostle Paul writes to the church in Rome, "For in it the righteousness of God is revealed from faith to faith; as it is written, 'The just shall live by faith.'"[128] So, confess Jesus as your righteousness and go live in faith. It is not that you are righteous on your own, but because of Jesus God considers you righteous. Soak in that incredible grace of God.

Sixth. Confess, "Jesus, you are my holiness." God called his church to be holy. "Just as he chose us in him before the foundation of the world, that we should be holy and without blame before him in love."[129] Confess Jesus as your holiness.

Seventh. Confess, "Jesus, you are my glory." The Bible says that "all have sinned and fall short of the glory of God."[130] But our Lord Jesus has become that glory for us. It is by the work of Jesus and by receiving him as our Lord that we can partake in God's glory. Confess Jesus as your glory today.

126. 2 Sam 22:33.
127. Jer 23:6.
128. Rom 1:17.
129. Eph 1:4.
130. Rom 3:23.

Prayer at the Mercy Seat

The top portion of the Ark is called the atonement cover.[131] It is also called 'the mercy seat.' It is a place where the High Priest sprinkled the blood of the animal sacrifice for the remission of sins once a year.

You have proceeded from the bronze altar to the atonement cover step by step. Finally you have come to the throne. Here, you now freely ask for the desires of your heart and for the work God has entrusted to you. Pray the following seven prayers following the ripple prayer order.

First. Pray for yourself and your family. What is your desire for yourself and your family? Pray that prayer. Do not limit God.

Second. Pray for your spiritual family. What does God want to do with your church? What is your role in it? Pray for those things freely.

Third. Pray for your siblings and relatives. Call out their names and bless them. If forgiveness is needed, forgive and ask for God's favor and intervention on their behalf. Remember how Abraham interceded for Lot.[132] Be the Abraham for your loved ones.

Fourth. Pray for your neighbors and friends. There is no accidental relationship! God has given you a specific group of people to love and mature with through that relationship. Love them through your prayer. Freely bless them with your intercession.

Fifth. Pray for your city. Where you live is your mission field. Represent Jesus in the place God has placed you.

131. Exod 25:17–22.
132. Gen 18:16–33.

Bless the city and ask God to move in your city. Pray for city officials and public workers. Pray for order and peace in the city.

Sixth. Pray for your country. Pray that your country will represent Christ to the rest of the world. As I traveled throughout the world, it broke my heart to see America represented by Hollywood and its sinful lifestyle. One godly man from Australia politely but firmly requested of me, "Sir, please pray that America and her sinful lifestyle will not influence our young people!" Let's pray that God will heal this land to represent him once again.[133]

Seventh. Pray for all the people on earth. God is weeping over the nations that still reject him. Pray that God will open doors for mission work to be activated. The apostle Paul requested intercession on his behalf for the doors of opportunity to open for evangelism.[134] Let's pray that God's mighty work will be accomplished all over the world.

Since God is the God of order, he detests babbling.[135] After finishing all the courses of the tabernacle prayer designed to cover the cross of Christ, purification, the Holy Spirit, and our praise to him, you can be more assured of a closer relationship with God. As the priest took those steps to approach God, you can approach God in an orderly manner each day and experience the greater presence of God and his favor.

133. 2 Chr 7:14 "If my people who are called by my name will humble themselves, and pray and seek my face, and turn from their wicked ways, then I will hear from heaven, and will forgive their sin and heal their land."

134. 1 Cor 16:9.

135. Matt 6:7.

Day 14: To Pray Like Jesus

An insight to meditate on: You will prosper in all things!

God's word to heartify: "Beloved, I pray that you may prosper in all things and be in health, just as your soul prospers." 3 John 2

A question to ask: Is your prayer life deepening? What part of prayer that was lacking the most in your life up to this point? How can you get closer to God through prayer today?

Let us pray: Let's pray through the final three stages of the Tabernacle Prayer.

Item	Today in Prayer	Your Prayer
Incense Altar	Prayer of thanksgiving and adoration to God.	1. 2. 3.
Ark of the Covenant	Pray before Christ as represented in the Ark: Word of God Jesus as the Bread of life. Jesus as the Resurrection.	1. 2. 3.
Mercy Seat	Prayer of intercession for all aspects of your life.	1. 2. 3.

Part III: To Join Jesus in His Prayer

DAY 15: PRAYER IS INTERCESSION—KNOCK

"Knock, and it will be opened to you . . ."

—LUKE 11:9B

"I believe that the kingdom of Heaven is taken by force. God doesn't mind if we bang on the door to heaven sometimes, asking him to listen to what we have to say."

—BONO OF U2

K NOCK, AND it will be opened to you.

An Intercessory Prayer

As a new Christian, you approach prayer as the means by which you can receive from God, which is petitionary prayer. In time, you begin to mature and desire more. The newness of your experience is no longer as strong, so you may think you are slipping. What is actually happening is that you are being weaned spiritually from your infant formula and are being prepared for adult food. Then you must enter into spiritual communion and fellowship with Christ through devotional prayer. And from there you enter *intercessory prayer*!

Knock. "So I say to you, ask, and it will be given to you; seek, and you will find; knock, and it will be opened to you."[1] The third level of prayer is intercession in which you share the burden of Christ for a person, circumstance or need anywhere in the world.

Jesus in intercession. Let me give you a picture of intercession by Jesus. Jesus prayed earnestly, "Then his sweat became like great drops of blood falling down to the ground."[2] Intercessory prayer is not difficult to understand. It is difficult to do. It involves experiencing brokenness with the Father over those who continually rebel against him. How many of us will experience this kind of fervent intercession?

You long for Pentecost in your life and in your churches, but there is no Pentecost without Gethsemane and a cross. How do you become more mature in your prayer life? By praying. When you do not feel like praying is precisely the time you ought to pray. There are no shortcuts to prayer.

Why not accept God's invitation to become an intercessor? Don't allow yourself to become satisfied with shallow, self-centered praying. Stay with God in prayer until he leads you to pray at the level he wants.

Why is intercession necessary?

Because you are an ambassador for Christ—you represent Jesus Christ in your own circle of influence. There is no one else. A famous pastor cannot fill your shoes. He does not belong to that circle of influence. God sent you there to represent him. You are a little Jesus to them. Listen to what

1. Luke 11:9.
2. Luke 22:44.

the Word of God says, "Now then, we are ambassadors for Christ, as though God were pleading through us: we implore you on Christ's behalf, be reconciled to God."[3]

Being a Christian is not only a privilege but also a responsibility. Everywhere you go, you are now responsible to represent the kingdom of God as an ambassador of Christ.

Testimony. Many years ago I was doing my quiet time and received a very distinct word from the Lord. It was 'Cambodia.' "Lord, why Cambodia?" You see, I am geographically challenged. I did not even know where this country was. But the burden for Cambodia increased in my heart. So I sought after Cambodian refugees in the government housing project in the Los Angeles area, planted a church, and also started helping out with the Cambodia mission effort, thinking that that is what God wanted me to do. He wanted more!

In 2002, I was at Peum Trung, Cambodia, with my summer mission team, preaching at the leper's village church. This village has been there for hundreds of years. Children are born healthy, but due to long term exposure to the disease, they themselves become lepers. Talk about a generational curse! After my preaching, the local missionaries were treating little children for minor cuts and administering simple medicine. One little girl had a deep cut on her knee and was being treated. I walked over and was observing this. The missionary gave her a piece of candy and she held it tight bracing herself for what was about to take place next. You see, there is no medicine there. So what they do is rub alcohol over the cut in an effort to kill the germs. But, of course, a little girl does not know that. She thought that they were killing her and she let out a scream! She was

3. 2 Cor 5:20.

crying but was holding on to her candy. That was her prize for going through hell. I found a new use for candy that day. To my surprise and dismay, the missionary and her mother were rejoicing at her screams. "What is wrong with these people? They are so cruel!" That's what I thought. But that thought changed quickly.

The next patient was a little boy. He had exactly the same cut on his knee. That's common for young kids who are running around the jungle all day without shoes. This brave boy was holding on to his candy and was getting ready for the rubbing alcohol treatment. I braced myself for a good scream. The alcohol was poured, but he had no response. He was smiling and looking at his candy. "What a brave little boy," I thought. But the truth of what was happening hit me. "He is a leper!" He's got it already. This little boy does not feel pain because he's got his dad's sickness. I broke down. I ran out of the church and found the biggest palm tree and wept uncontrollably. "God, it is not fair! What kind of future would this little boy have now? Why can't a rich American church come and do something about this?" I was half complaining and half interceding for the boy. Then the Holy Spirit spoke, "Why don't you stop the leprosy forever in Peum Trung?" God gave me and my church a project that day: WOLP—War on Leprosy & Poverty. We needed to buy a twenty-acre plot of land, isolate the children, and start a boarding school for them. Also, we would give these leper families chickens to raise for profit and for nourishment. All these projects needed money. We had to raise almost $300,000.

When I came back to America, God already had a man of peace in place. One Christian businessman, a godly elder of another church, shared that God had been convicting him to help this project with the money he had been saving. He gave $100,000 in cash! With that first seed offering, our people gave sacrificially and God provided the total amount needed for the project.

My man of peace, Elder David Kim, later went to Cambodia with me and God convicted him to retire and start a business venture in Vietnam to continuously support this school. He obeyed. Praise the Lord.

The school is built and there are about ninety students learning the Bible and growing in the Lord. They are getting a top-notch education. There is no running water or electricity in that area, so we had to dig a well and install a generator, in order to give them an American-style toilet and shower, and also to teach computer skills. They are going to be the leaders of that community. Also, with a partnership with another mission agency there, a high school and a Bible college are being built in an effort to plant three hundred churches all over Cambodia. Only God can do that!

By the way, the name of this school is 'Bright Future School.' My complaint to God had been, "What kind of future would this little boy have?" Well, a bright future—in Christ!

Because you are called by God as a kingdom priest. God chose you and your generation to be his royal priesthood. "You are a chosen generation, a royal priesthood, a holy nation, his own special people, that you may proclaim the praises of him who called you out of darkness into his marvelous light."[4]

---

4. 1 Pet 2:9.

The whole process of sacrifice worship at the tabernacle, shedding the blood of an animal, bringing it to the Most Holy Place, and sprinkling the blood at the Mercy Seat can be summed up in one word—Intercession. That's the role of a priest. So, that's now your role as a Christian.

Testimony. Are you the first one in the family to be saved? The Bible says that, "You and all your household will be saved."[5] I have been confessing this verse for most of my Christian life and have reaped the harvest.

My father accepted Christ three months before he passed on after a few decades of intercession. My mother was the first one to accept Christ and is now a prayer warrior attending an early morning prayer service each day to cry out and pray. My first sister, Nancy, is a missionary to Mongolia. My second sister, Somi, for whom I prayed for sixteen years, is a lay pastor. My third sister, who accepted Christ after her cancer, is now healed and serves God. Finally, my brother, for whom I prayed for twenty-three years, was born-again and serves at a men's ministry called 'Father School' as a lay leader. The Word of God is true, "You and all your household will be saved." Hallelujah! Intercession works!

Let me tell you a story about Nancy, my first sister. She was born-again and attended a church but was very much self-focused as a Christian. I prayed for her that she would break out of her shell and be more other-centered. She lived in a different city, and one Sunday she made a visit to my church. I was glad to see her at the service, but with her being the oldest and me being the youngest of five children, there was an obvious generational and cultural gap. After

5. Acts 11:14b.

the service, I offered a benediction for the congregation and was walking out to the back to greet the people. As I was passing her, the Holy Spirit spoke to me. He said, "Now go over to Nancy and lay your hand on her and pray for her." "But, Lord, she is my oldest sister. I cannot lay my hand on her. That is not culturally acceptable, Lord," I said. I had to struggle on the spot for few seconds. But I obeyed. I walked up to her and asked. "Nancy, can I pray for you?" Of course she said, "Yes."

What happened afterwards changed her life and mine. As soon as my hand touched her forehead, she fell under the power of God and broke out into a very loud tongue. She immediately got into this incredible intercessional prayer. There was only one problem—her church taught that speaking in tongues was from the devil. Well, her theology changed that day, and her worldview changed as well. She experienced the touch of the Holy Spirit in a mighty way. A few years later, she confessed that God was putting Mongolia in her heart. And after a few years of training she went to Mongolia as a missionary. She sold her home and totally committed herself to see the young people of Mongolia being saved and sent out as missionaries through the Silk Road. She is no longer a self-absorbed Christian, but an other-centered intercessor. Praise God!

Are you ready to knock? It will be opened to you.

Day 15: To Join Jesus in His Prayer

An insight to meditate on: You are an ambassador of Christ and a royal priesthood!

God's word to heartify: "But you are a chosen generation, a royal priesthood, a holy nation, his own special people, that you may proclaim the praises of him who called you out of darkness into his marvelous light." 1 Pet. 2:9

A question to ask: What can you do today to represent Christ in your own circle of influence? Write them down. Ask God for wisdom. Who are you interceding for right now? Ask God to lay some souls upon your heart.

Let us pray: You are going to make a list of doors to knock on. Write down a prayer agenda or names of people you are going to intercede for and start praying.

- Myself:
- Family:
- Spiritual Family:
- Siblings/Relatives:
- Neighbors/Friends:
- City:
- Nations/Political leaders:
- World:

DAY 16: WARFARE PRAYER

"For the weapons of our warfare are not carnal but mighty in God for pulling down strongholds."

—2 COR 10:4

"Life is war . . . our weakness in prayer is owing largely to our neglect of this truth. Prayer is primarily a wartime walkie-talkie for the mission of the church as it advances against the powers of darkness and unbelief."

—JOHN PIPER

You are a soldier of Christ!

Christian life happens in the war zone. Jesus said he will build his church by the gates of Hades but it shall not prevail against the church.[6] Why would God build his church next to gates of hell? God does this so the church can see millions upon millions entering there everyday. We are called to fight for souls. John Piper is right when he called prayer a wartime walkie-talkie. Too many churches in America have turned prayer into a "Club Med" intercom!

Church, let's go back to our rightful place—the war zone—in prayer! You need to take part in binding the strong man over America who has been deceiving Christians to accept prayerlessness as a norm, acceptable, and at times seemingly a more civilized form of Christianity.[7]

Apostle Paul challenges us to "Fight the good fight of faith, lay hold on eternal life, to which you were also called."[8] War rages on, soldiers of Christ—let's put up a good fight!

There are several levels of intercession.

Level one: circumstantial intercession. It's what I call, the "I have to intercede" level. This is where all Christians begin to learn about intercession. You have to because you are in a situation to pray for something or someone. God puts you through some boot camp type of experience to get the taste of this level of intercession.

Make every problem into an opportunity to intercede. Do you have financial problems right now? Turn that into an opportunity to intercede and learn about prayer. How can you overcome that situation? What is the cause? How can I prevent it? Seek the Lord and ask God for wisdom and

---

6. Matt 16:18.
7. Luke 11:20–21.
8. 1 Tim 6:12a.

his intercession into your problem. You can overcome with God's help.

There is a reason why you are there. Are you in a crisis? Why do you think you are in that circumstance? You guessed it. You are there to intercede—you are the chief intercessor of that situation. God will send you through these boot camp experiences over and over again until you learn how to cope and successfully learn to overcome. Then, of course, you go to the next level. Sorry, the journey does not end.

CIPFY? That means "Can I Pray for You?" Use this question effectively and you will become an excellent circumstantial intercessor. Everyone desires prayer—rich or poor, educated or uneducated, tall or short, skinny or chunky, PC users or Mac users— because you are all created in God's image, and there is a deep yearning to connect with God.

Once I was traveling on a plane sitting next to "the Fonz"—Henry Winkler from the 1970s sitcom, "Happy Days." Wow. He was my hero when I was growing up. He would say, "Aay!" and all the pretty girls would flock to him. What a guy! For a twelve-year-old Korean immigrant boy watching this on TV this man was it. Well, sitting next to him I asked, "CIPFY?" And he did have a prayer request about his family. Wow, Fonz had a prayer request. Now, I am certain that everyone has prayer requests. I had him sign my Bible so I can pray for him, and he graciously signed his name for me. What a guy. He is still my man!

At times God will put you in more serious situation than that. Let me tell you a story.

Testimony. I supported my college education by serving as a resident janitor at a church. I was studying philosophy at UC Berkeley at the time, training to be a pastor. It was an exciting time. I wanted to disciple people. I met this brother named Jim[9] who was into all kinds of wrong things. However, he recently accepted Christ. He said he had no place to go, so I invited him to stay at my little room in that church. It was a section of a Sunday school room. We had no shower facility there and I had one single bed. We managed to stay together somehow and I was teaching him the Bible and trying to disciple him. He would do well for a while, then he would lose it. Jim would come home late at night all drunk, breaking my stuff in the room and cutting himself with broken glass. Thank God I did not have any valuables at the time. As far as the cutting went, he was cutting his own skin, so I was fine with that! One morning I woke up to find my bed soaked in his blood. There was too much evil in him for him to deal with.

After about a month, a more serious incident took place. Around 2:00 or 3:00 am, a bunch of local Oakland gang members broke into my room demanding to know where Jim was. "I have not seen him all day," I replied honestly. By the look in their eyes, they were ready to kill somebody. They explained that Jim got totally drunk and had broken into his own home and beaten his mother almost to death. She was in hospital but would not tell the authorities who had done that to her. But they knew and they wanted to kill him. They said, "We have a code of honor in this gang. We don't allow a dirt bag like that to live." It was very critical that I found him first. The race was on. I called up an ex-big boss, who was in his late thirties, who had just been saved a little earlier. I pleaded with him to find Jim first.

9. Not his real name.

We searched for him for a few hours. We found him at the International House of Pancakes. I was relieved to find him but I wasn't ready for what was going to take place.

An evil spirit in him completely took over his personality. When I challenged him to repent and make it right with his mother, he said, "That old woman deserves to die!" His eyes were glowing with evil. I had no option but to bring him to the Lord under the cross, I mean literally. The ex-big boss was a really a big man physically. I told him to grab him and bring him to church. I locked up the main sanctuary and put Jim under the cross and put the big man on his guard. Jim wasn't going anywhere. I told Jim, "Brother, I am going to intercede on your behalf. You were bought with the blood of Christ, so you and I are brothers in Christ. So, your mom is like my mom. What you did to her is what you did to my mom. I am going to sit next to you under the cross to intercede for you to repent. Please pray with me." With that I went into a desperate intercession for my friend, my brother in Christ who needed deliverance. A spiritual war was upon us.

Jim was laughing and chanting obscenities about his mother. I kept pushing forward in my intercession. After awhile there was silence. Then I heard Jim's scream, "Bob, please come and pray for my arms. My arms!" He was on the carpet rolling back and forth. "What's going on, Jim?" I asked. He started crying. This is what happened. From the time I started praying for Jim, a numbing sensation and then pain started to invade from the top of his fingers down to his elbow. When I touched his arms they were as cold as ice. He was dying, and he was in great pain. I knew what God was doing. He was punishing those hands that struck his mother—the same mother who still loved him so much that she refused to tell the authorities about him. He was shouting by this time, "Please, pray for me!" Now I had the upper hand. I told him, "Wait a minute! There is no rush." I started dealing with him.

I put all the cards on the table. I said, "Jim, are you ready to repent?" "Yes, I repent!" he shouted back. I wasn't satisfied. I told him again. "Say it sincerely, Jim." I had a great time—it was fun! What satisfaction there was hearing him repenting and promising to go back to his mother, pledging to love her and take care of her the rest of her life. By the time he repented and made a covenant before God much time had passed. Once my objective was achieved, I took both of his hands and interceded for them. An amazing thing took place. He was instantly healed at that moment. Praise God!

Of course, he kept his promise. A few years later on January 21, 1984, I was walking down the aisle to be married to a beautiful sister I met at Berkeley and my best man following me was none other than Jim, the one who was healed and was living a brand new life in Christ. That's what intercession can do! It transforms lives.

Are you in difficult circumstances right now? Take that as an opportunity to intercede to God and experience his glory. Amen!

Level two: committed and called intercession. This is the "I want to intercede" level. Sometimes you have the desire to intercede, not necessarily due to circumstances, but as a result of your commitment and call. I pray for my family constantly, because I am committed to their wellbeing. I have been writing prayers in my diary for many decades. I pray using the ripple prayer model.

On the first day of the month, I write an intercessory prayer for my wife Jenny. The second day, my first daughter, Elisa, the love of my life. The third day, my son, Stephen, the hope of my life. The fourth day, my second daughter, Patty, the joy of my life. And the ripple prayer list is made. In this way, my loved ones will have at least twelve written-out intercessions for them each year. When I pass on, our kids will be able to read intercessions I did for them each month. It's easy. My kids have a date designated for them. Intercession is cumulative. Keep banking prayers of blessing for your kids. God will honor those prayer letters of credit at the bank of heaven.

Level three: career intercession. This is the "I must intercede or I will die" level. This spiritual 'seal team' of intercessors is very unique. They literally feel like they are going to die if they do not log in at least eight or ten hours of prayer each day. I have to admit, I am not at this level. But I met many such career intercessors at the International House of Prayer of Kansas City.

As I was celebrating my twenty-fifth spiritual birthday last year on August 3, I decided to go to the center of America and pray for this country for several days. The center of America, geographically, is at Kansas City. There were several hundred career intercessors at work around the clock seeking God and praying for America at this prayer center. I was in the third heaven. I enjoyed their ministry tremendously. What a party! Thank you Lord for these prayer warriors.[10]

In the New Testament, these career intercessors played a major role at the birth of Jesus. Simeon and Anna, were

10. Web site for International House of Prayer: www.fotb.com.

the first ones to the recognize Jesus as Messiah and offer up a prophetic prayer.[11] Their job was fasting and praying all day in the temple, interceding on behalf of God's people. For some people such intensive prayer is unthinkable. Yet for some it is their career choice. If you have this unbearable burden and passion for prayer, you may be one of them. Talk to your spiritual leaders about it and get guidance.

Testimony. Dr. Cho was sharing at a private meeting about his intercessory experiences. Dr. Cho said that one time he was ministering in a Muslim country. For whatever reason, though he was officially invited, he was warned not to share the Gospel by the local authorities. The stadium was full of people and the police chief in charge strongly warned him not to share the Gospel, but instead to just share good stories. He reminded Dr. Cho that converting a Muslim to Christianity in his country is a capital crime, punishable by death. He said that there were many armed guards all around the podium. Wow. What would you have done in such a situation?

Dr. Cho prayed and went up to the podium and started his sermon by saying, "God loves you so much, he sent his only begotten Son Jesus to die on the cross for you! The only way to heaven is by accepting him as your Lord and Savior." He went out and swung the Gospel sword with all his might. At the end of that message, all the guards and the leader of the local authorities gave their lives to Christ and became born-again. What an incredible testimony!

I asked him, "Weren't you afraid?" He smiled and told me his secret. "I have 3,000 full time intercessors praying for me around the clock, fasting and crying out to God at

11. Luke 2:25–39.

the Prayer Mountain in Korea." The power of God comes through their intercession! Then I realized that Dr. Cho was not running on just some spiritual battery that needs to be recharged again and again. He is totally plugged into the main power source of heaven through these intercessors.

A spiritual war is upon you. Are you ready to fight?

Day 16: To Join Jesus in His Prayer

An insight to meditate on: You are a solider of Christ!

God's word to heartify: "Fight the good fight of faith, lay hold on eternal life, to which you were also called and have confessed the good confession in the presence of many witnesses." 1 Tim 6:12

A question to ask: Where are you now spiritually? Are you ready to enlist in the Army of God and fight on the front line? What can you do today to make this happen?

Let us pray: Pray for those people you know who need deliverance. Let's seek God for their wellbeing and a break though in their lives.

DAY 17: THE LORD'S PRAYER

"Thy kingdom come . . ."

—MATT 6:10

"For daily need there is daily grace; for sudden need, sudden grace, and for overwhelming need, overwhelming grace."

—JOHN BLANCHARD

Let's memorize the Lord's Prayer.

"Our Father in heaven, hallowed be your name. Your kingdom come, your will be done on earth as it is in heaven. Give us this day our daily bread and forgive us our debts, as we forgive our debtors. And do not lead us into temptation, but deliver us from the evil one. For yours is the kingdom and the power and the glory forever. Amen." [12]

Our Father in heaven. Prayer not directed to God is merely a talking to self. It won't be heard by God. As a Christian, you pray to the triune God: the Father, the Son and the Holy Spirit. God's name is 'Jehovah (Yahweh)' and it is a redemptive name in the unchanging covenant relationship with humanity. It is his name that bestows salvation.

Hallowed be your name. As a Christian, when you take on the holiness of God and live according to his holiness, you glorify God's name. "But when he sees his children, the work of my hands, in his midst, they will hallow my name, and hallow the Holy One of Jacob, and fear the God of Israel."[13] (Refer to Day 10—seven redemptive names of God.)

Your kingdom come. God's kingdom refers to his authority over the world. His kingdom is filled with righteousness, peace, joy and forgiveness that drive away illness and evil spirits. [14] Jesus Christ brought the kingdom of God through the Cross. Therefore, all those in God's kingdom receive eternal life and salvation.

12. Matt 6:9–13.

13. Isa 29:23.

14. Matt 12:28, "But if I cast out demons by the Spirit of God, surely the kingdom of God has come upon you."

Five Blessings Due to the Cross[15]

1. Forgiveness of sin and the gift of righteousness: justification.

2. The Holy Spirit: sanctification. [16]

3. Divine health and healing: edification.

4. Deliverance from curses: edification.

5. Eternal kingdom of heaven: glorification.

We long for the day that our Lord Christ Jesus will return to the earth and rule over again with his glory.[17]

Someone humorously said, "Thy kingdom come—*not*—die and come to the kingdom!" You represent God's kingdom. When you go to someone who is sick, you bring the kingdom of God with you—the healing touch of Jesus Christ. With that in mind, pray, "Let God's kingdom come into my life!"

Your will be done on earth as it is in heaven. God's will toward man is always good and merciful. God's greatest desire for us is our salvation. God "desires all men to be saved and to come to the knowledge of the truth."[18] God desires the best for all of us. He knows us the best so his will is the best for us. So, do not question his will for you.

15. Dr. Cho's teaching on the Lord's Prayer at the Church Growth International, Seoul, Korea, 1992.

16. Rom14:17, "For the kingdom of God is not eating and drinking, but righteousness and peace and joy in the Holy Spirit."

17. Rev 22:20, "Surely I am coming quickly." Amen. Even so, come, Lord Jesus!

18. 1 Tim 2:4.

King David recognized that God knew all about him. "O Lord, you have searched me and known me. You know my sitting down and my rising up; you understand my thought afar off. You comprehend my path and my lying down, and are acquainted with all my ways. For there is not a word on my tongue, but behold, O Lord, you know it altogether."[19]

Give us this day our daily bread. The daily bread encompasses all that you need to live each day. As you pray for what you need and what your neighbors need, God answers and blesses abundantly. King David sings this truth onto the Lord, "The Lord is my shepherd; I shall not want."[20]

Forgive us our debts, as we forgive our debtors. You must confess your sins and your failures to God on a daily basis. You have been given the privilege to pray for the cleansing of your sin in the name of Jesus Christ. If you have been forgiven by God, you must also extend the hand of forgiveness to those who commit wrongs against you.

> Take heed to yourselves. If your brother sins against you, rebuke him; and if he repents, forgive him. And if he sins against you seven times in a day, and seven times in a day returns to you, saying, "I repent," you shall forgive him.[21]

Do not lead us into temptation. You must pray that God will keep you safe from the temptations of Satan and worldly, carnal desires. You must ask God to keep you holy. But if you fail and sin against God, then you must be

19. Ps 139:1–4.
20. Ps 23:1.
21. Luke 17:3.

washed clean with the blood of Jesus Christ and ask God to strengthen your faith against failing again.

Jesus warns his disciples, "Watch and pray, lest you enter into temptation. The spirit indeed is willing, but the flesh is weak."[22] How true is his warning to us all!

But deliver us from the evil one. You must pray and ask God to protect you from the schemes of the enemy. When you make that prayer of protection, God will keep you safe and deliver you from evil.

> "No temptation has overtaken you except such as is common to man; but God is faithful, who will not allow you to be tempted beyond what you are able, but with the temptation will also make the way of escape, that you may be able to bear it." [23]

For yours is the kingdom and the power and the glory forever. Only God deserves the ultimate everlasting glory and worship. You must worship and glorify God who saved you and answers your prayer. "For the Son of Man will come in the glory of his Father with his angels, and then he will reward each according to his works."[24]

Amen. Amen is a confirmation of your desire and faith concerning the prayer you have offered to God. "For all the promises of God in him are yes, and in him Amen, to the glory of God through us."[25]

22. Matt 26:41.
23. 1 Cor 10:13.
24. Matt 16:27.
25. 2 Cor 1:20.

Day 17: To Join Jesus in His Prayer

An insight to meditate on: Jesus taught us to pray orderly and systematic way.

God's word to heartify: The Lord's Prayer.

A question to ask: Is God's kingdom manifesting in your life?

Let us pray: Let's memorize the Lord's prayer together and pray meditating on each of the points of this study. Write it in your own words.

The Lord's Prayer	Your Prayer
Our Father in heaven,	
Hallowed be your name.	
Your kingdom come.	
Your will be done on earth as it is in heaven.	
Give us this day our daily bread.	
And forgive us our debts, as we forgive our debtors.	

And do not lead us into temptation,	
but deliver us from the evil one.	
For yours is the kingdom and the power and the glory forever.	
Amen.	

DAY 18: FASTING PRAYER[26]

"This kind can come out by nothing but prayer and fasting."

—MARK 9:29

"As we begin to focus upon God, the things of the Spirit will take shape before our inner eyes."

—A.W. TOZER

Fasting is a normal part of Christian discipline!

Fasting is a voluntary and deliberate abstinence from food for the purpose of concentrated prayer. It is not some esoteric spiritual practice for the special few. It should be a normal part of Christian life.

Jesus expects you to fast. Christ taught on fasting by saying, "When you fast."[27] Make a note here that he did not say, "If you fast." Jesus expected his disciples to fast. As a

26. Cho, *Prayer That Brings Revival*, 113.

27. Matt 6:16.

matter of fact, fasting was a well-accepted form of spiritual discipline for Jews and those who practice other forms of religion. Pharisees fasted regularly as part of their religious rituals.

Jesus fasted foty days. Jesus fasted and prayed before he started his public ministry. "Jesus, being filled with the Holy Spirit, returned from the Jordan and was led by the Spirit into the wilderness, being tempted for forty days by the devil. And in those days he ate nothing, and afterward, when they had ended, he was hungry."[28] Notice that Jesus was filled with the Holy Spirit as he began fasting. But after his fasting, "Jesus returned in the power of the Spirit to Galilee, and news of him went out through all the surrounding region."[29]

From the Scripture quoted above, we can deduce that being full of the Holy Spirit does not necessarily cause one to walk in the power of the Spirit. I believe the way into power, especially in prayer, is to fast and pray. After the fast, Jesus returned in the power of the Spirit. Spiritual power is gained through fasting prayer!

Then why didn't Jesus' disciples fast? "The disciples of John came to him, saying, 'Why do we and the Pharisees fast often, but your disciples do not fast?'" And Jesus said to them, 'Can the friends of the bridegroom mourn as long as the bridegroom is with them? But the days will come when the bridegroom will be taken away from them, and then they will fast.'"[30] Jesus wanted his disciples to fast but not in a ritualistic way.

28. Luke 4:1–2.
29. Luke 4:14.
30. Matt 9:14–15.

Relationship not ritual. The word of Jesus makes this one point. Fasting is not about keeping up with religious regulations, but about a relationship with God. He radically redefines what was known of fasting up to that point into something more personal and relational. The most intimate relationship one can experience in this life would be that between a bride and her bridegroom. Jesus uses that image to describe fasting. You should never fast to fulfill some sort of religious requirement.

Since our bridegroom has been taken away, these last two thousand years have been a season of fasting for his bride. This season will continue until he comes back. Bride of Christ, get ready to fast.

Apostle Paul fasted. Apostle Paul's ministry also began with three days of fasting and prayer.[31] Paul testifies to the Corinthian church that he proved his ministry by his spiritual discipline: "In watching, in fasting."[32]

In public gatherings, the early church fasted and prayed in order to know the will of God. The church at Antioch after fasting and praying heard from the Holy Spirit to send Paul and Barnabas as their missionaries, church planters to the neighboring cities.[33]

When Paul and Barnabas started their ministry, they started teaching about fasting prayer and implemented it as a church discipline. "So when they had appointed elders in every church, and prayed with fasting, they commended them to the Lord in whom they had believed."[34]

31. Acts 9:9.
32. 2 Cor 6:5.
33. Acts 13:1–3.
34. Acts 14:23.

The previous verses show that fasting prayer is a vital part of gaining direction from the Holy Spirit. Fasting combined with prayer caused the early church to have clarity of mind and spirit to establish its foundation.

Fasting is a precious opportunity to get closer to God—to be nurtured and to be sent out with a clear direction and a goal.

How does fasting work? The desire for food is basic to all living creatures. It is one of the strongest motivational forces at work in the body. If you can combine this intense natural desire with your spiritual desire for communion with God, then what results is a much greater intensity in focus and force. By combining these two desires, the intensity of your petition to God multiplies. It is not simple addition. It is multiplication. It is like a spiritual explosion!

Because God responds to humility. The point is not to be hungry, but to be humble. When you fast God responds to your humility. In the Old Testament, God fights for the Israelites every time they humble themselves by fasting and repenting. "If my people, which are called by my name, shall humble themselves, and pray, and seek my face, and turn from their wicked ways; then will I hear from heaven, and will forgive their sin, and will heal their land."[35]

Breaking anointing. Fasting can break the bands of wickedness. It can cause the oppressed to go free. It can bring total and complete deliverance. It really is a supernatural work of the Holy Spirit.

Testimony. Many years ago, I was in an extended fast. At that time God gave me three names and how I needed to minister to them. However, I was perplexed, because I was at a prayer retreat center going through something

35. 2 Chr 7:14.

like my thirtieth day of fasting. I said, "God, do I have to do it now?" The answer was, "Yes." I had to drive a total of one thousand miles roundtrip in order to obey him. Was it worth it? Oh, yes!

The first person I visited was the president of a Christian publishing company. We met on an airplane one time and became good friends. The word God gave to him was, "Be faithful and I will increase you by double!" We talked a bit and I had to go, I had a long journey ahead of me. The next person was an elder who was struggling with a gambling problem. It was a firm warning, "Go back to your first love. This is a final notice." He understood what I was talking about. He cleaned up his life and still serves at his church faithfully. Hallelujah!

The third person I had to visit was my mother-in-law. When I arrived at her house, late in the afternoon, I rang the bell and shouted, "Mom, I am here!" Then I heard someone responding, "OK, I am coming!" I waited and waited but no one came out. "It's quite strange," I thought, because she usually runs out and greets me. I went through the backyard and the back door was open. I went in and started calling for her. But no one was there. The house was empty and there was a presence of an evil spirit. All the hair on my body went up.

At that time I remembered reading about how Pastor John Wimber had to make holy water quickly out of tap water to anoint a place. So, I quickly got some tap water in a cup and prayed over it. I started sprinkling it all over the house. When I was finally done, Mom came home. Of course, she was bit surprised by my sudden visit. I did not tell her about what happened, but just had great fellowship.

At the end of our conversation, I wanted to bless her with a prayer. When I laid my hand over her, she broke out into a beautiful tongue. She wept and testified, "I have been wanting to receive a gift of tongues since I was a young girl. Now, God answers my prayer!" What a testimony! Something in the heavens broke through. Praise God!

Oh, and what happened to that Christian publishing company? Many years later I was invited to that company's new building dedication service. I was sitting in the audience, when Pastor Jack Hayford (who is a board member of that company) made a comment in passing about how this new building is twice larger than their previous one. The Lord reminded me of the word I had for this company. I think my good friend forgot about my brief talk with him, because even for me it was a very distant memory. But God never forgets. He spoke and it is so!

Do you need a breakthrough? Try fasting!

Day 18: To Join Jesus in His Prayer

An insight to meditate on: Fasting is a normal Christian spiritual discipline!

God's word to heartify: "If my people, which are called by my name, shall humble themselves, and pray, and seek my face, and turn from their wicked ways; then will I hear from heaven, and will forgive their sin, and will heal their land." 2 Chr 7:14

A question to ask: What can you do to schedule more fasting days in your life?

Let us pray: If you are not media fasting already, please start now. Let's pray for more of God's anointing and an activation of his gifts in our lives.

Part IV: Listen and Obey

DAY 19: GOD SPEAKS

*"He who has an ear, let him hear
what the Spirit says to the churches."*

—Revelation 3:6

*"Prayer is surrender—surrender to the will of God
and cooperation with that will."*

—E. Stanley Jones

You can have a dialogue with God!

Prayer is a dialogue. Prayer is a dialogue, not a monologue. Listening to him is very much part of prayer as well as speaking to him. To listen to God's voice, you must have the proper attitude. Jesus said, "If anyone wills to do his will, he shall know concerning the doctrine, whether it is from God or whether I speak on my own authority."[1] Jesus teaches us the importance of a willing attitude toward the will of God. If you are not willing to do his will, you cannot hear God's voice clearly. It's really quite logical. Why should God speak to someone who is not willing to obey?

Listen. To pray effectively, you must listen to God as well as speak. "He who has an ear, let him hear what the

1. John 7:17.

Spirit says to the churches."[2] Thus, having an ear to hear is to have the capacity to understand with an attitude of obedience. If you don't sincerely want to do his will, you will not have the capacity to listen to God.

God is speaking. There are at least ten different ways in which God speaks. Now this is an area that needs some elaboration:

One: Bible. God speaks to us through the Bible. It is one of the major ways in which God reveals himself to us. "The Word of God is living and active, sharper than any double edged sword."[3] Yes, his words are living and active.

Open your Bible each morning ready to hear. He is speaking through the Bible.

Two: Voice. The Bible makes it clear that you can hear what God says. "He who belongs to God hears what God says."[4] Father Abraham heard from the Lord as he began his faith journey. Moses heard from God in the burning bush. The apostle Paul heard God's voice on the road to Damascus.

Three: Prayer. God wants to communicate to you through prayer, which is the key teaching of this book.

Four: Vision. "The word of the Lord came to Abram in a vision."[5] God communicates through visions. When I was a second-year college student, I had a vision about publishing books with my youth pastor who was a seminary student at the time. Although, it did not make sense at the

2. Rev 3:6.
3. Heb 4:12.
4. John 8:47a.
5. Gen 15:1.

time, I kept that vision in my heart and kept cultivating my relationship with him and my writing skills.

Many years went by, and my youth pastor, after finishing his fifth Phd in theology, became the chaplain at Korea's largest seminary. And he started a publishing house called Faith & Understanding. Up to this date, I have published five books through them with more on the way. God is amazing!

Five: Prophecy. We need more prophets to rise up from our churches and bring the Word of God to us. The Bible warns us not to "treat prophecies with contempt."[6] Prophecy is a powerful way in which God confirms what he will do in the future. One time, Cindy Jacobs prophesied over me and said, "Many Buddhist temples will shut down because of your ministry." As I was listening to her, I thought to myself, "OK, Cindy now that is way off! I have a ministry in Los Angeles, not in Southeast Asia!"

That was seven years ago. Today, we have a sizable mission project in Cambodia. Our goal is to plant three hundred churches in the Kampong Cham region. I think Buddhist temples will shut down because of our ministry. Cindy was onto something. It's called a prophetic gift. Thank God for prophets among us!

Six: The Holy Spirit. The Holy Spirit actually spoke to the church in such a clear way in the book of Acts that they put quotation marks around what he said.[7] Unless it is verbatim, quotation marks cannot be used. The Holy Spirit is a person. So, rightfully, what he said was recorded verbatim with quotation marks.

6. 1 Thess 5:20.
7. Acts 13:1–3.

Testimony. One time I was visiting a different city, and had a lunch appointment set with my friend who had a ministry there. I was listening to some praise music, minding my own business and enjoying myself. Then the Holy Spirit spoke to me. He said, "Write this down. 'I give and I take away!'" What? I did not know how to respond to him. I wrote it down on the back of my hand verbatim anyways while I was driving. I was thinking to myself, "Well, you are God. You can do whatever you want and say whatever you want to say!" Still questioning, "But what does 'I give and I take away' mean?"

I arrived at my friend's house and was ready to go out and have a nice lunch. But when I got there he had invited all of his elders to his house without my permission for me to minister to them. I was hungry and upset. I didn't want to preach!

This is what my friend said: "When I got off the phone with you this morning, I had a sense of urgency to call all of my elders and tell them to skip work and come. I told them that I have this Asian pastor who's going to bring the Word of God to you." How could I refuse? So I just read the back of my hand, "God gives and God takes away!" Based on that, I preached for about two hours. After my preaching session, I was starving and was ready for lunch. But one of the elders stopped our lunch plan and shared his testimony.

You see, God called him to a full time ministry fifteen years ago. God spoke to him to give up everything and become a pastor, but he refused. He told God, "I just started this business and I need to build it up little bit, Lord!" Seven years went by and God spoke to him again about a full time ministry. He refused again. His reasoning was that his kids are growing up and he needs to be there and provide for them.

Then he said, "This morning in my quiet time, God came to me and spoke these words to me. 'I gave you everything but if you don't obey, I am going to take away everything!'" He was shocked. At that precise moment the phone rang from his pastor informing him about that day's meeting with me. He came to that meeting with fear and trembling. And when I opened my mouth, the first word was, "God gives and God takes away!" He was so awed by what had taken place, he fell on his knees before my friend and me, asking for our blessing. At that very place, he was giving his life to become a full time servant. We wept together as we were praying for that elder.

When the Holy Spirit speaks every word counts!

Seven: The church. According to Acts 13, God speaks through the body of Christ—his church. As God gives a specific vision for a person, each church receives a specific call to accomplish for the expansion of his kingdom.

Eight: God-given desires. God puts a desire in our heart to fulfill his will. "Delight yourself also in the Lord, and he shall give you the desires of your heart."[8] Many times, the term 'desires' is used in a negative context. But the psalmist makes it clear that some desires are from the Lord.

Nine: Dreams. Dreams are legitimate way in which God communicates his will to us. Do not treat your spiritual dream with contempt. "Joseph had a dream,"[9] and even though no one believed in him, Joseph never lost faith in God who communicated to him in a dream.

8. Ps 37:4.
9. Gen 37:5.

Ten: Circumstance. God speaks through special circumstances. Sometimes, you may not even be looking for them. Simon, who happened to be in Jerusalem at the time of Jesus' crucifixion, ended up taking the cross of Jesus. What an incredible honor! He was at the right place at the right time.

God is speaking. When you listen to him you will know what he is up to. The Bible says that the Lord does nothing, unless he reveals his secret to his servants the prophets.

Day 19: Listen and Obey

An insight to meditate on: You can have a dialogue with God!

God's word to heartify: "He who has an ear, let him hear what the Spirit says to the churches." Rev 3:6

A question to ask: God is talking to you, are you listening?

Let us pray: Let's pray to him as if we are talking to our loved ones. Let's practice dialogue prayer. Speak and Listen. Have fun!

DAY 20: LISTEN AND OBEY

"Teach me to do your will, for you are my God; your Spirit is good. Lead me in the land of uprightness."

—Ps 143:10

"If I had to do it all over, I would do more praying and less preaching."

—BILLY KIM

Listen and Obey!

Obedient listening. True listening is obedient listening. To listen to God is to obey him. True wisdom from above is received by those who are prepared to obey it. The Bible says that to obey is better than sacrifice.

Leanne Payne writes, "To listen in prayer for the voice of the Lord is to find the mind of Christ; it is to gain transcendent wisdom, a wisdom that includes understanding, guidance, knowledge, exhortation, and consolation."[10]

Jesus tells this parable to his disciples, "But what do you think? A man had two sons, and he came to the first and said, 'Son, go, work today in my vineyard.' He answered and said, 'I will not,' but afterward he regretted it and went. Then he came to the second and said likewise. And he answered and said, 'I go, sir,' but he did not go. Which of the two did the will of his father?"[11] What is your answer to his question? Jesus demands obedient listening from his followers.

Oswald Chambers once said that the proof that your old self is crucified with Christ is the amazing ease with which the life of God in you enables you to obey the voice of Jesus Christ. If you do not insist on your ways, then obedience becomes easier—but never completely automatic.

Time to respond. Dr. Cho writes: "I see one great fault in American services. American pastors deliver fantastic messages to the congregations; but right afterward the people are dismissed and leave. They are not given time to bear the fruit those messages have brought to life. They receive all

10. Payne, *Listening Prayer: Learning to Hear God's Voice and Keep a Prayer Journal*, 125.

11. Matt 21:28–31.

the spoken words of the message, but have no time to pray through it, to get that word so implanted that it becomes a part of them."[12]

It is not for information's sake that I preach the Gospel. It is about transformation.

Wallace Heflin Jr. in his book entitled, *Hear the Voice of God*, offers this prayer for hearing. You should read this prayer out loud for yourself.

Prayer for Hearing[13]

"Dear God, in the name of Jesus, I believe you for your people today. Many are desirous of hearing your voice, of knowing your will, your plan and your purposes. God, each of us needs direction. Speak to them, Lord. Reveal yourself to them. Let ears be open to you. Speak to this people by day and by night as only you can; and let them be sensitive enough to hear your voice and be willing to obey. Let there be hearing! Let there be an understanding! I take authority over doubt and unbelief. I take authority over confusion. I take authority over uncertainty. Let there be clarity! Let there be sensitivity! I believe you for it, oh God. In the name of Jesus, Amen!"

ASAYH! Cindy Jacobs writes the following. "In the late '70s and early '80s, the Lord began to train me in obedience. I once heard Dr. David Yonggi Cho say the key to this success was that he 'prayed and obeyed.' I didn't know his secret."[14]

12. Cho, *The Fourth Dimension, Volume One*, 66.
13. Heflin, *Hear the Voice of God*, 208–9.
14. Jacobs, *The Voice of God*, 44.

When is a good time to obey? The time to obey is ASAYH! No, it's not a Hebrew word, but an acronym for "As Soon As You Hear." Do not hesitate. Do not ask God for more time to think about it. The time to obey God is as soon as you hear. As soon as you are certain that God has spoken to you, that is the time that you need to move. Put it in action. That's what faith is all about.

Also, you have to know that only you can obey. It is not other's responsibility to obey your call. Let me say in the apostle Paul's word, "Therefore, I urge you, brothers, in view of God's mercy, to offer your bodies as living sacrifices, holy and pleasing to God, this is your spiritual act of worship."[15]

Benefits of Obeying. The Bible says, "If you are willing and obedient, you will eat the best from the land."[16] If you want the best from the land, start obeying him!

Only those who love God can obey him. It's really a heart issue. Moses states, "when you and your children return to the Lord your God and obey him with all your heart and with all your soul according to everything I command you today."[17] Also, "Jesus replied, "If anyone loves me, he will obey my teaching. My Father will love him, and we will come to him and make our home with him."[18]

When you obey, you get the blessing. "Blessed rather are those who hear the word of God and obey it."[19]

Don't miss out on your blessing! Listen and obey him!

15. Rom 12:1.
16. Isa 1:19.
17. Deut 30:2.
18. John 14:23.
19. Luke 11:28.

Day 20: Listen and Obey

An insight to meditate on: You get the blessing when you obey!

God's word to heartify: "Blessed rather are those who hear the word of God and obey it." Luke 11:28

A question to ask: Are you obeying God?

Let us pray: Let's pray that we will obey God and his words.

DAY 21: CAN YOU TARRY WITH ME AN HOUR?

"My soul is exceedingly sorrowful, even unto death: tarry ye here, and watch with me."

—Matt 26:38

"I want a life of greater, deeper, truer prayer."

—Archbishop Tait

Would you tarry with Jesus?

God-sized prayer. Mahesh Chavda writes, "Just as Jesus prays and intercedes for us day and night without ceasing, so should we intercede for the lost and for laborers for the harvest. This harvest is global in magnitude. Therefore it requires corporate prayer on the same magnitude. When a wheat farmer wants to harvest half an acre of grain, he only needs to plan on bringing in a limited amount of machinery and just a few workers. However, when he wants to harvest 100,000 acres in a day, he has to plan to bring in a large number of machines, many skilled operators and an army of workers, or all is lost."[20]

Pray big. I pray that you will take a God-sized task for your life. God is always doing God-sized work! He wants to save the whole world and he needs you to join him in that effort. The bigger the workload, the bigger the intercession. That's how it works spiritually.

Martin Luther prayed big. Martin Luther described his prayer life. "In a typical day I am charged with the pastorate of three congregations. I teach regularly at the seminary. I have students living in my house. I am writing three books. Countless people write to me. When I start each day, therefore I make it a point to spend an hour in prayer with God." Now that's making prayer a priority![21]

You have learned the following types of prayers in the last twenty days.

Ask—Prayer is Petition!

Topical Prayer

Ripple Prayer

Seek—Prayer is Devotion!

Tabernacle Prayer

Knock—Prayer is Intercession!

Warfare Prayer

The Lord's Prayer

Fasting Prayer

20. Chavda, *The Hidden Power of Prayer and Fasting*, 147–48.
21. Smith, *Intercessors & Pastors*, 70.

I am finishing my forty day fast as I finish writing this book. I have been praying for you that as you study this book you will be set free from prayerlessness and become a powerful prayer warrior.

I pray that you will experience the *Prayer Driven Life* all the days of your life here on earth.

Let's heartify: "My soul is exceedingly sorrowful, even unto death: tarry ye here, and watch with me." Matt 26:38

Let's pray! You can choose any form of prayer. Let's spend some time praying now. Let's experience greater, deeper, and truer prayer together.

Appendices

Appendix 1: Resource—Heartifying Verses

Day 1: "Pray without ceasing." 1 Thess 5:17

Day 2: "Be anxious for nothing, but in everything by prayer and supplication, with thanksgiving, let your requests be made known to God." Phil 4:6

Day 3: "Seek first the kingdom of God and his righteousness, and all these things shall be added to you." Matt 6:33

Day 4: "There is therefore now no condemnation to those who are in Christ Jesus . . ." Rom 8:1

Day 5: "Ask, and it will be given to you; seek, and you will find; knock, and it will be opened to you." Matt 7:7

Day 6: "If you then, being evil, know how to give good gifts to your children, how much more will your Father who is in heaven give good things to those who ask him!" Matt 7:11

Day 7: "If you abide in me, and my words abide in you, you will ask what you desire, and it shall be done for you." John 15:7

Day 8: "The righteous cry out, and the Lord hears, and delivers them out of all their troubles." Ps 34:17

Day 9: "You shall be witnesses to me in Jerusalem, and in all Judea and Samaria, and to the end of the earth." Acts 1:8b

Day 10: "I love those who love me, and those who seek me diligently will find me." Prov 8:17

Day 11: "And do not be conformed to this world, but be transformed by the renewing of your mind, that you may prove what is that good and acceptable and perfect will of God." Rom 12:2

Day 12: "Christ has redeemed us from the curse of the law, having become a curse for us." Gal 3:13a

Day 13: "Do you not know that you are the temple of God and that the Spirit of God dwells in you?" 1 Cor 3:16

Day 14: "Beloved, I pray that you may prosper in all things and be in health, just as your soul prospers." 3 John 2

Day 15: "But you are a chosen generation, a royal priesthood, a holy nation, his own special people, that you may proclaim the praises of him who called you out of darkness into his marvelous light." 1 Pet 2:9

Day 16: "Fight the good fight of faith, lay hold on eternal life, to which you were also called and have confessed the good confession in the presence of many witnesses." 1 Tim 6:12

Day 17: "Our Father in heaven, hallowed be your name. Your kingdom come. Your will be done on earth as it is in heaven. Give us this day our daily bread. And forgive us our debts, as we forgive our debtors. And do not lead us into temptation, but deliver us from the evil one. For yours is the kingdom and the power and the glory forever. Amen." The Lord's Prayer.

Day 18: "If my people, which are called by my name, shall humble themselves, and pray, and seek my face, and turn from their wicked ways; then will I hear from heaven, and will forgive their sin, and will heal their land." 2 Chr 7:14

Day 19: "He who has an ear, let him hear what the Spirit says to the churches." Rev 3:6

Day 20: "Blessed rather are those who hear the word of God and obey it." Luke 11:28

Day 21: "My soul is exceedingly sorrowful, even unto death: tarry ye here, and watch with me." Matt 26:38

Appendix 1: Resource—The Tabernacle Prayer Table

Item	The Old Testament	Today in Prayer	Ref. Verses
Bronze Altar	The sacrifice of animal and the burnt offering.	Through the blood of Jesus Christ we are saved. Pray the prayer of thanksgiving.	Rom 5:9, 10 Eph1:7
Basin	Washing of hands and feet of priests before entering the temple.	Prayer of purification is offered through repentance.	Ps 32:5 1 John 1:9
Lampstand	Made out of pure gold. Seven candle sticks to light the temple interior.	The seven spirit of the Holy Spirit (Rev. 1:4)	Isa 11:2 John 8:12
Showbread Table	It is showbread presented in the temple.	Pray to be able to stand on his word.	Ps 119:18 2 Tim 3:16, 17
Incense Altar	It is burning twenty-four hours.	Prayer of thanksgiving and adoration to God.	Eph 6:18 I Thess 5:16–18

Ark of the Covenant	The tablets of the Ten Commandments, a jar of manna, and Aaron's staff which budded is kept in there.	Pray before Christ as represented in the Ark: Stone Tablets—the Word of God. Manna—Jesus as the bread of life. Aaron's Staff—Jesus as the resurrection.	John 1:14 John 6:15 John 11:25, 26
Mercy Seat	The top of the Ark where the Glory of God manifests.	Pray the desires of your heart. Pray the prayer of intercession for all aspects of your life.	Psalm 148:13 I Tim. 2:1–4

Bibliography

Barrier, Roger. *Listening to the Voice of God.* Minneapolis, MN: Bethany House, 1998.

Chavda, Mahesh. *The Hidden Power of Prayer and Fasting.* Shippensburg, PA: Destiny Image, 1998.

Cho, David Y. *A Bible Study for New Chrisitans.* Seoul: Seoul Logos, 1997.

———. *Born to Be Blessed.* Seoul: Seoul Logos, 1993.

———. *How Can I Be Healed.* Seoul: Seoul Logos, 1999.

———. *How to Pray.* Seoul: Seoul Logos, 1997.

———. *Prayer: Key to Revival.* Waco, TX: Word Books, 1984.

———. *Prayer That Brings Revival: Interceding for God to Move in Your Family, Church, and Community.* Lake Mary, FL: Charisma House, 1998.

———. *Praying with Jesus.* Altmonte Springs, FL: Creation House, 1987.

———. *Revelation: Visions of Our Ultimate Victory in Christ.* Lake Mary, FL: Creation House, 1991.

———. *Salvation, Health & Prosperity.* Altamonte Springs, FL: Creation House, 1987.

———. *Solving Life's Problems.* Plainfield, NJ: Logos International, 1980.

———. *Spiritual Leadership for the New Millennium.* Seoul: Seoul Logos, 1999.

———. *The Apocalyptic Prophecy.* Lake Mary, FL: Creation House, 1990.

——. *The Fourth Dimension, Volume One*. Gainesville, FL: Bridge-Logos, 1979.

——. *The Holy Spirit, My Senior Partner: Understanding the Holy Spirit & His Gifts*. Lake Mary, FL: Charisma House, 1989.

——. *The Leap of Faith*. South Plainfield, NJ: Bridge, 1984.

——. *The Nature of God: Who is God . . . Really?* Lake Mary, FL: Charisma House, 2001.

Heflin, Wallace H., Jr. *Hear the Voice of God*. Hagerstown, MD: McDougal, 1997.

Jacobs, Cindy. *The Voice of God*. Ventura, CA: Regal, 1995.

Kennedy, Nell L. *Dream Your Way to Success: The Story of Dr. Yonggi Cho and Korea*. Plainfield, NJ: Logos International, 1980.

Payne, Leanne. *Listening Prayer: Learning to Hear God's Voice and Keep a Prayer Journal*. Grand Rapids, MI: Baker Books, 1994.

Schuller, Robert, and Paul Y. Cho. *Expand Your Horizon: How to Make Your Faith Work!* Melbourne, FL: Dove Christian, 1985.

——. *Prayer: My Soul's Adventure with God: A Spiritual Autobiography*. Nashville, TN: Thomas Nelson, 1995.

Smith, Eddie, and Alice Smith. *Intercessors & Pastors: The Emerging Partnership of Watchmen & Gatekeepers*. Houston, TX: SpiriTruth, 2000.

Wangerin, Walter, Jr. *Whole Prayer: Speaking and Listening to God*. Grand Rapids, MI: Zondervan, 1998.

Warren, Rick. *The Purpose Driven Life*. Grand Rapids, MI: Zondervan, 2002.

CPSIA information can be obtained
at www.ICGtesting.com
Printed in the USA
BVHW040758170122
626422BV00017B/420

9 781610 976022